Daily Bible Study 101:
Daily Devotional

DAILY BIBLE STUDY 101: DAILY DEVOTIONAL
By Reggie Casaus

BRIDAN PUBLISHING
Post Office Box 25
Kingston, TN 37763 U.S.A.
bridanpublishing.com

All rights reserved. No part of this book may be reproduced or transmitted in any form or by any means—graphic, electronic, mechanical, including photocopying, recording, taping, Web distribution, or by any information storage and retrieval system, or otherwise—without prior written permission from the author, except for the inclusion of brief quotations in a review.

Sales of this book without a front cover may be unauthorized. If this book is coverless, it may have been reported to the publisher as "unsold or destroyed" and neither the author nor the publisher may have received payment for it.

Copyright © 2018 by Bridan Publishing

All Scripture quotations are taken from the Authorized King James Version of the Bible.

Cover art © Shutterstock www.shutterstock.com

Interior art by VisionRun.com

Cover design by Jeff Jansen

Library of Congress Control Number: 2018902490

Paperback ISBN-13: 978-0-9979638-0-9
Ebook ISBN-13: 978-0-9979638-1-6

       Religion / Christian Life / Devotional

Printed in the United States of America

Dedicated to all Christian martyrs.

And they shall not teach every man his neighbor, and every man his brother, saying, Know the Lord: for all shall know me, from the least to the greatest.

Hebrews 8:11

Daily Bible Study 101:
Daily Devotional

The words of the LORD *are pure words: as silver tried in a furnace of earth, purified seven times. Thou shalt keep them, O* LORD, *thou shalt preserve them from this generation for ever.*

Psalm 12:6-7

Table of Contents

Forward xi

January 13

February 29

March 45

April 61

May 77

June 93

July 109

August 125

September 141

October 157

November 173

December 189

"I believe the Bible is the best gift God has ever given to man. All the good from The Savior of the world is communicated to us through this Book."

Abraham Lincoln

FOREWARD

A familiar phrase is *society is going to hell in a handbasket*. Today we live in an age where political correctness is at war with Biblical correctness. In too many situations evil is considered good, and good is considered evil.

We live in a time when Christianity is mocked by celebrities, and Hollywood films and television programs blaspheme the LORD'S name without guilt, shame, or reservation.

Like the ancient Israelites who sacrificed their children to the fires of Baal, America is also guilty of murdering its children. Abortion is no longer considered evil, but good.

In addition, the pornography industry is a billion dollar business. However, the price is hefty considering it has wrecked many homes, lead to destructive addictions, and ruined lives.

Like Lot's wife—who disobeyed God and could not control her impulse to look back and was turned into a pillar of salt—many people refuse to give up the sin in their lives. For example, the abuse of drugs—including opioids and alcohol—have become major epidemics.

Many American families are dysfunctional. It has become the norm for too many men to abandon their families and refuse to pay child support. In addition, parents often lack basic parenting skills; instead of being a parent, they are more focused on being their child's friend. Unfortunately, over half of all marriages end in divorce within 5-10 years.

Not only has God been kicked out of homes, He has also been kicked out of society. The results have been devastating. Violent crimes are on the rise. Massacres and shootings now occur in places once deemed safe such as schools, churches, movie theaters, concerts, baseball parks, and work places. Prisons and jails are overcrowded. There are not enough police officers to fight the upswing of crimes. Police officers are being ambushed and murdered. Mobs have turned to the streets to vent their frustrations, oftentimes injuring and killing others and burning businesses to the ground.

How can we end all of this? Do we need to pass more laws? Do we need fewer guns? Do we need more prisons? Do we need to increase security? Do we need more taxes? Do we need a bigger government?

The answer is found in II Chronicles 7:14, which states, *If my people, which are called by name, shall humble themselves, and pray, and seek my face, and turn from their wicked ways; then will I hear from heaven, and will forgive their sin, and will heal their land.*

When we recognize that the Bible—one of God's greatest gifts to man—is the answer to all of our problems, only then will we have true revival in our homes, communities, and nation.

This daily devotional was written to encourage individuals to read the entire Bible from the Book of Genesis to the Book of Revelation within one entire year. It is a great companion to *Daily Bible Study 101: Questions & Answers*, a book that contains 20 multiple choice questions that coincide with a daily reading schedule that helps the reader to read the entire Bible within one year.

One final note, in addition to reading the Bible, one must also heed its warnings and do what it says in order to receive true success.

Reggie Casaus

JANUARY

1

And I will put enmity between thee and the woman, and between thy seed and her seed; it shall bruise thy head, and thou shalt bruise his heel.

Genesis 3:15

This is God's first promise of his plan of redemption for fallen man. This plan of redemption is so that all of God's people will be free from the bondage of sin.

Today's Reading: Genesis 1–3

January

2

And Enoch walked with God: and he was not; for God took him.

Genesis 5:24

When the *Rapture* happens, it will be very similar to Enoch's translation to heaven.

Today's Reading: Genesis 4–7

3

And Noah began to be an husbandman, and he planted a vineyard: And he drank of the wine, and was drunken; and he was uncovered within his tent.

Genesis 9:21

Instead of being drunk with liquor that kills, become intoxicated with the indwelling power of the Holy Spirit that brings new life.

Today's Reading: Genesis 8–11

January

4

Now the LORD had said unto Abram, Get thee out of thy country, and from thy kindred, and from thy father's house, unto a land that I will shew thee:
Genesis 12:1

Abraham was such a man of faith he believed there was nothing God could not do. We as believers in God must also have faith that He will someday bring us home to our promised land.

> **Today's Reading: Genesis 12–15**

5

And when Abram was ninety years old and nine, the LORD appeared to Abram, and said unto him, I am the Almighty God; walk before me, and be thou perfect.
Genesis 17:1

El Shaddai is Hebrew for "God Almighty." Jesus said, "...with God all things are possible" (Matthew 19:26). Begin each day by asking the all-powerful God to make the impossible things in your life possible.

> **Today's Reading: Genesis 16–18**

January

6

So Abraham prayed unto God: and God healed Abimelech, and his wife, and his maidservants; and they bare children.
Genesis 20:17

In your daily prayers do not forget to pray for your family, friends, neighbors, country, other nations, and—yes—even your enemies.

> **Today's Reading: Genesis 19–20**

7

And he said, Lay not thine hand upon the lad, neither do thou any thing unto him: for now I know that thou fearest God, seeing thou hast not withheld thy son, thine only son from me.
Genesis 22:12

Jehovahjireh (Genesis 22:14 KJV) in Hebrew means, "The Lord will provide." God would never want us to sacrifice a child. To abort, abuse, or murder any child is the work of the Devil.

> **Today's Reading: Genesis 21–23**

January

8

And he said, O LORD God of my master Abraham, I pray thee, send me good speed this day, and shew kindness unto my master Abraham.
Genesis 24:12

If you want to be successful in the eyes of the Lord, then seek His guidance.

> Today's Reading: Genesis 24–25

9

And he dreamed, and behold a ladder set up on the earth, and the top of it reached to heaven: and behold the angels of God ascending and descending on it.
Genesis 28:12

We are not to worship angels. In addition, when a saved person dies, he does not become an angel; on the contrary, a believer is set over the angels in heaven.

> Today's Reading: Genesis 26–28

January

10

And Jacob did so, and fulfilled her week: and he gave him Rachel his daughter to wife also.

Genesis 29:28

Jacob ended up with two wives; this goes against God's plan that there should be only one husband and only one wife in a marriage. If a husband and wife truly love each other, they will spend so much time pleasing each other they won't have the time or desire to have an affair.

Today's Reading: Genesis 29–30

11

And when he saw that he prevailed not against him, he touched the hollow of his thigh; and the hollow of Jacob's thigh was out of joint, as he wrestled with him.

Genesis 32:25

God gave Jacob a limp after wrestling with the angel because he wanted Jacob to be dependent upon Him for strength. Consequently, God may use an illness or another loss to bring us back to Him.

Today's Reading: Genesis 31–32

January

12

Then Jacob said unto his household, and to all that were with him, Put away the strange gods that are among you, and be clean, and change your garments:

Genesis 35:2

What foreign gods do you have in your home? Get rid of any astrological items, Buddha statues, satanic images, and pornographic material. Remove anything that is offensive to God.

> Today's Reading: Genesis 33–35

13

And Joseph dreamed a dream, and he told it his brethren: and they hated him yet the more.

Genesis 37:5

Dreams are still one of the ways in which God can make his way known to man. The indwelling of the Holy Spirit is also another means by which God communicates to man. However, the Bible is still God's primary form of revelation.

> Today's Reading: Genesis 36–38

January

14

And it came to pass, as I lifted up my voice and cried, that he left his garment with me, and fled out.

Genesis 39:17

Joseph was falsely accused of attempted rape and thrown into prison. Even though others may tell lies about us, God knows the truth.

> **Today's Reading: Genesis 39–41**

15

And he said, Behold, I have heard that there is corn in Egypt: get you down thither, and buy for us from thence; that we may live, and not die.

Genesis 42:2

Just as Jacob sent out his sons to Egypt to bring back bread, so must the church. If unbelievers are unwilling to come to church and receive Christ, then the church must bring them the Bread of Life.

> **Today's Reading: Genesis 42–44**

January

16

Now therefore be not grieved, nor angry with yourselves, that ye sold me hither: for God did send me before you to preserve life.

Genesis 45:5

It is a true blessing to witness someone who was once an evil person, but came to know the Lord, repented, and is now a new creation in Christ.

> Today's Reading: Genesis 45–47

17

Unstable as water, thou shalt not excel; because thou wentest up to thy father's bed; then defiledst thou it: he went up to my couch.

Genesis 49:4

Jacob's firstborn son, Reuben, lost his place of honor because of adultery with his step-mother's maid and father's concubine. A Christian must be on guard when tempted. In fact, God gives us the power to overcome all temptation and a means to escape.

> Today's Reading: Genesis 48–50

January

18

Come now therefore, and I will send thee unto Pharaoh, that thou mayest bring forth my people the children of Israel out of Egypt.

Exodus 3:10

Notice God sends Moses back to Egypt. Likewise, God commands us to do the same. He wants us to go back and tell others the *Good News* of Jesus Christ.

Today's Reading: Exodus 1–3

19

And he said, Cast it on the ground. And he cast it on the ground, and it became a serpent; and Moses fled from before it.

Exodus 4:3

Jesus said one of the signs that will accompany believers is they will pick up snakes and not be hurt (Mk 16:15-18). This verse has often been taken out of context. Remember, Jesus also said when tempted by the Devil, "thou shalt not tempt the Lord thy God" (Matt. 4:7). In other words, don't handle deadly snakes.

Today's Reading: Exodus 4–6

January

20

For they cast down every man his rod, and they became serpents: but Aaron's rod swallowed up their rods.
Exodus 7:12

Believers cannot deny the existence of demonic power. Therefore, one must be careful not to confuse demonic miracles for the power of God.

Today's Reading: Exodus 7–9

21

For I will pass through the land of Egypt this night, and will smite all the firstborn in the land of Egypt, both man and beast; and against all the gods of Egypt I will execute judgment: I am the LORD.
Exodus 12:12

The Egyptians believed in polytheism (many gods). Thus, the ten plagues were a sign to all that God is the true God over all of heaven and earth.

Today's Reading: Exodus 10–12

January

22

And it came to pass, when Pharaoh would hardly let us go, that the LORD slew all the firstborn in the land of Egypt, both the firstborn of man, and the firstborn of beast: therefore I sacrifice to the LORD all that openeth the matrix, being males; but all the firstborn of my children I redeem.
Exodus 13:15

The mighty hand of God that slew the firstborn of Egypt is the same nail-scarred hand that delivers us from death.

Today's Reading: Exodus 13–15

23

Moreover thou shalt provide out of all the people able men, such as fear God, men of truth, hating covetousness; and place such over them, to be rulers of thousands, and rulers of hundreds, rulers of fifties, and rulers of tens:
Exodus 18:21

God never intended for a pastor to do all the work of a local church. Instead, God has equipped the church with gifts such as missionaries, prophets, evangelists, pastors, and teachers to help the pastor reach the lost.

Today's Reading: Exodus 16–18

January

24

And ye shall be unto me a kingdom of priests, and an holy nation. These are the words which thou shalt speak unto the children of Israel.

Exodus 19:6

As holy people of God, we are to be sanctified—set aside for the Lord and separated from sin.

> Today's Reading: Exodus 19–21

25

Thou shalt not suffer a witch to live.

Exodus 22:18

Witchcraft and other occult practices are all abominations to the Lord. As a result, avoid astrology, Ouija boards, fortunetellers, and any other form of sorcery.

> Today's Reading: Exodus 22–24

January

26

And the LORD spake unto Moses, saying, Speak unto the children of Israel, that they bring me an offering: of every man that giveth it willingly with his heart ye shall take my offering.
Exodus 25:1-2

Out of respect for God, we should give cheerfully back to God what already belongs to Him. Moreover, it should not be done begrudgingly, but from the heart.

> **Today's Reading: Exodus 25–27**

27

But the flesh of the bullock, and his skin, and his dung, shalt thou burn with fire without the camp: it is a sin offering.
Exodus 29:14

Jesus also suffered outside the city gates for our sins, and we are told to go to him outside of the camp (Hebrews 13:12–13). The camp today is the world and all of its sinful pleasures. As Christians, we are following Christ to a pure and holy city beyond this world.

> **Today's Reading: Exodus 28–29**

January

28

See, I have called by name Bezaleel the son of Uri, the son of Hur, of the tribe of Judah: And I have filled him with the spirit of God, in wisdom, and in understanding, and in knowledge, and in all manner of workmanship,
Exodus 31:2-3

Pray that God would fill you with the Holy Spirit and empower you with spiritual gifts to do the will of God in your life.

> **Today's Reading: Exodus 30–32**

29

And it shall come to pass, while my glory passeth by, that I will put thee in a clift of the rock, and will cover thee with my hand while I pass by: And I will take away mine hand, and thou shalt see my back parts: but my face shall not be seen.
Exodus 33:22–23

No man has ever seen God's face and lived, yet we are commanded to continuously seek his face (Psalm 105:4), especially when we are face to face with the storms of life.

> **Today's Reading: Exodus 33–35**

January

30

And Moses called Bezaleel and Aholiab, and every wise hearted man, in whose heart the LORD had put wisdom, even every one whose heart stirred him up to come unto the work to do it:

Exodus 36:2

People can use their skills either to help or to hurt others. However, God's plan is that we would use our skills to help others and to further His kingdom.

Today's Reading: Exodus 36–38

31

Then a cloud covered the tent of the congregation, and the glory of the LORD filled the tabernacle.

Exodus 40:34

The Church must never compromise with the ways of the world. In other words, we must continue to love the sinner, but hate the sin.

Today's Reading: Exodus 39–40

FEBRUARY

1

If his offering be a burnt sacrifice of the herd, let him offer a male without blemish: he shall offer it of his own voluntary will at the door of the tabernacle of the congregation before the LORD.

Leviticus 1:3

Salvation involves three steps. First, the sinner must confess with his mouth that he is a sinner. Second, he must believe in his heart that Christ not only died for his sins, but also rose from the dead. Finally, he must receive Christ as his Lord and Savior.

Today's Reading: Leviticus 1–4

February

2

And it shall be, when he shall be guilty in one of these things, that he shall confess that he hath sinned in that thing:
Leviticus 5:5

Is there sin in your life keeping you from receiving God's blessing? If so, then pray now for God's forgiveness. God is ready and able to forgive you of *all* of your sins.

Today's Reading: Leviticus 5–7

3

And Moses said unto Aaron, Go unto the altar, and offer thy sin offering, and thy burnt offering, and make an atonement for thyself, and for the people: and offer the offering of the people, and make an atonement for them; as the LORD commanded.
Leviticus 9:7

In order to be reconciled back to God, our sins must be atoned. The blood of Jesus Christ atones for our sins, bringing us back to God.

Today's Reading: Leviticus 8–9

February

4

And Nadab and Abihu, the sons of Aaron, took either of them his censer, and put fire therein, and put incense thereon, and offered strange fire before the LORD, which he commanded them not. And there went out fire from the LORD, and devoured them, and they died before the LORD.

Leviticus 10:1-2

Jesus said when we pray we are not to use vain repetitions as the heathen do for they think they will be heard for their many words (Matt. 6:7). Instead, we should pray from the heart.

Today's Reading: Leviticus 10–12

5

When a man shall have in the skin of his flesh a rising, a scab, or bright spot, and it be in the skin of his flesh like the plague of leprosy; then he shall be brought unto Aaron the priest, or unto one of his sons the priests.

Leviticus 13:2

Leprosy caused lesions throughout the body that caused a foul odor when they burst. The leper's appearance became lion-like and hideous, and a person usually died a horrible death within nine years of becoming a leper as their flesh rotted away. As leprosy separated man from man, sin separates man from God.

Today's Reading: Leviticus 13

February

6

Thus shall ye separate the children of Israel from their uncleanness; that they die not in their uncleanness, when they defile my tabernacle that is among them.
                                              Leviticus 15:31

Cleanliness is next to Godliness. God gave the Israelites strict rules concerning hygiene. Modern medical science has confirmed that good hand washing alone can prevent the spread of many communicable diseases.

> **Today's Reading: Leviticus 14–15**

7

None of you shall approach to any that is near of kin to him, to uncover their nakedness: I am the LORD.
                                              Leviticus 18:6

We are to abstain from all forms of sexual immorality such as fornication, adultery, bestiality, homosexuality, incest, pornography, and prostitution. God warns us He will cast out nations that defile themselves through sexual immorality.

> **Today's Reading: Leviticus 16–18**

February

8

And thou shalt not glean thy vineyard, neither shalt thou gather every grape of thy vineyard; thou shalt leave them for the poor and stranger: I am the LORD your God.

Leviticus 19:10

God expects us to care for those in need. In fact, the church—not just the government—are to care for the poor, the orphans, and the widows.

Today's Reading: Leviticus 19–21

9

Speak unto the children of Israel, and say unto them, When ye be come into the land which I give unto you, and shall reap the harvest thereof, then ye shall bring a sheaf of the firstfruits of your harvest unto the priest:

Leviticus 23:10

Pay God first when you receive your wages. It isn't that God needs your money—He already owns everything. Giving back to God is a sign of your faith that God can meet all of your needs.

Today's Reading: Leviticus 22–23

February

10

Six years thou shalt sow thy field, and six years thou shalt prune thy vineyard, and gather in the fruit thereof; But in the seventh year shall be a Sabbath of rest unto the land, a Sabbath for the LORD: thou shalt neither sow thy field, nor prune thy vineyard.

Leviticus 25:3-4

The Israelites were to take one day off during the week, after six years they were to take a year off, and every 49 years they were to take two years off.

Today's Reading: Leviticus 24–25

11

I also will do this unto you; I will even appoint over you terror, consumption, and the burning ague, that shall consume the eyes, and cause sorrow of heart: and ye shall sow your seed in vain, for your enemies shall eat it.

Leviticus 26:16

There are more verses in the Bible dealing with curses rather than blessings. Thus, God wants to make it clear that we obey him.

Today's Reading: Leviticus 26–27

February

12

Take ye the sum of all the congregation of the children of Israel, after their families, by the house of their fathers, with the number of their names, every male by their polls; From twenty years old and upward, all that are able to go forth to war in Israel: thou and Aaron shall number them by their armies.

Numbers 1:2-3

The census made sure everybody was accounted for and that each person would be responsible for doing his fair share in the camp.

Today's Reading: Numbers 1–2

13

As for the sons of Merari, thou shalt number them after their families, by the house of their fathers; From thirty years old and upward even unto fifty years old shalt thou number them, every one that entereth into the service, to do the work of the tabernacle of the congregation.

Numbers 4:29-30

After the age of fifty our bodies usually start to weaken. This does not mean that we are to retire or quit; it simply means we are to slow down a little bit.

Today's Reading: Numbers 3–4

February

14

Then they shall confess their sin which they have done: and he shall recompense his trespass with the principal thereof, and add unto it the fifth part thereof, and give it unto him against whom he hath trespassed.

Numbers 5:7

Not only did the Israelites have to confess their sin, but they also had to make restitution to replace what had been lost.

> Today's Reading: Numbers 5–6

15

And the LORD spake unto Moses, saying, Take it of them, that they may be to do the service of the tabernacle of the congregation; and thou shalt give them unto the Levites, to every man according to his service.

Numbers 7:4-5

God expects us to care for those in the ministry. It is our duty as Christians to make sure that we meet the *needs*, not splurges, of God's faithful ministers.

> Today's Reading: Numbers 7

February

16

Or whether it were two days, or a month, or a year, that the cloud tarried upon the tabernacle, remaining thereon, the children of Israel abode in their tents, and journeyed not: but when it was taken up, they journeyed.

Numbers 9:22

Learn to be patient and wait for God to answer your prayers. His answers and timing are always perfect.

Today's Reading: Numbers 8–10

17

Send thou men, that they may search the land of Canaan, which I give unto the children of Israel: of every tribe of their fathers shall ye send a man, every one a ruler among them.

Numbers 13:2

The children of Israel failed to go into the Promised Land because they feared the giants living in the land. What fear do you have in your life keeping you from the promises of God?

Today's Reading: Numbers 11–13

February

18

And the LORD said unto Moses, How long will this people provoke me? and how long will it be ere they believe me, for all the signs which I have shewed among them?

Numbers 14:11

When fear replaces faith in God in our churches it causes disharmony and disunity.

> Today's Reading: Numbers 14–15

19

Thus speak unto the Levites, and say unto them, When ye take of the children of Israel the tithes which I have given you from them for your inheritance, then ye shall offer up an heave offering of it for the LORD, even a tenth part of the tithe.

Numbers 18:26

Ministers are also responsible for giving back to God. They are to set an example for the rest of the church members to follow.

> Today's Reading: Numbers 16–18

February

20

So they smote him, and his sons, and all his people, until there was none left him alive: and they possessed his land.
Numbers 21:35

God ordered the Israelites to slay Og, the king of Bashan, and his people because He did not want their pagan beliefs and vile worship practices, which included sexual immorality and child sacrifices, to corrupt the holy nation of Israel.

> Today's Reading: Numbers 19–21

21

And it came to pass on the morrow, that Balak took Balaam, and brought him up into the high places of Baal, that thence he might see the utmost part of the people.
Numbers 22:41

Beware of the error of Balaam, which includes ministers who distort the Word of God to become wealthy.

> Today's Reading: Numbers 22–24

February

22

Phinehas, the son of Eleazar, the son of Aaron the priest, hath turned my wrath away from the children of Israel, while he was zealous for my sake among them, that I consumed not the children of Israel in my jealousy.

Numbers 25:11

Phinehas used a spear to kill an Israelite male and his Midianite harlot. The message is clear: God did not tolerate fornication then, and neither does He tolerate it today.

> Today's Reading: Numbers 25–26

23

The one lamb shalt thou offer in the morning, and the other lamb shalt thou offer at even;

Numbers 28:4

The time of Jesus' death was at 3 p.m. This was also the same time of the day that the Passover lamb was to be slain. The animal sacrifices were not enough to atone for sin; only the precious blood of Jesus can bring atonement for our sins.

> Today's Reading: Numbers 27–29

February

24

If a man vow a vow unto the LORD, or swear an oath to bind his soul with a bond; he shall not break his word, he shall do according to all that proceedeth out of his mouth.

Numbers 30:2

Despite popular opinion today, God expects us to keep our promises, especially our marriage vows.

Today's Reading: Numbers 30–31

25

Now the children of Reuben and the children of Gad had a very great multitude of cattle: and when they saw the land of Jazer, and the land of Gilead, that, behold, the place was a place for cattle;

Numbers 32:1

These tribes were supposed to settle on the other side of the Jordan River. Similarly, when carnal Christians pursue their own selfish interests they fall short of receiving God's full blessings.

Today's Reading: Numbers 32–33

February

26

And among the cities which ye shall give unto the Levites there shall be six cities for refuge, which ye shall appoint for the manslayer, that he may flee thither: and to them ye shall add forty and two cities.

Numbers 35:6

Jesus Christ is our city of refuge. He shelters us from judgment for our sins. It is only through Christ that we can escape the second death and avoid going to hell.

Today's Reading: Numbers 34–36

27

The LORD your God which goeth before you, he shall fight for you, according to all that he did for you in Egypt before your eyes;

Deuteronomy 1:30

If you expect to win a fight, then choose the side God is for because in the end He always comes out the winner.

Today's Reading: Deuteronomy 1–2

February

28

But charge Joshua, and encourage him, and strengthen him: for he shall go over before this people, and he shall cause them to inherit the land which thou shalt see.
                                    Deuteronomy 3:28

Seek out the people who are like Joshua in your own church—men and women dedicated to God's Word. Encourage, equip, and allow them to use their spiritual gifts to edify the church and you.

Today's Reading: Deuteronomy 3–4

MARCH

1

Moreover the LORD thy God will send the hornet among them, until they that are left, and hide themselves from thee, be destroyed.
Deuteronomy 7:20

God fights for nations that love Him and keep His commandments. Likewise, He destroys nations that do not love Him and keep His commandments.

Today's Reading: Deuteronomy 5–7

March

2

And now, Israel, what doth the LORD thy God require of thee, but to fear the LORD thy God, to walk in all his ways, and to love him, and to serve the LORD thy God with all thy heart and with all thy soul,

Deuteronomy 10:12

Jesus was referring to this verse, as recorded in Luke 10:27, to let us know God wants all of us—our hearts, souls, strengths, and minds. God also desires that we love Him and our neighbors as ourselves. This is more important than offerings and sacrifices.

Today's Reading: Deuteronomy 8–10

3

Behold, I set before you this day a blessing and a curse.

Deuteronomy 11:26

There are more Scripture verses in the Bible addressing curses than blessings. This is because God desires us to live holy and pure lives, and He lets us know there are consequences for our actions.

Today's Reading: Deuteronomy 11–13

March

4

Thou shalt not sacrifice unto the LORD thy God any bullock, or sheep, wherein is blemish, or any evilfavouredness: for that is an abomination unto the LORD thy God.

Deuteronomy 17:1

God wants us to give Him our best, unlike Cain who did not give the best from his harvest. Giving back to God is a sign of faith that God can meet all of our needs.

Today's Reading: Deuteronomy 14–17

5

When thou goest out to battle against thine enemies, and seest horses, and chariots, and a people more than thou, be not afraid of them: for the LORD thy God is with thee, which brought thee up out of the land of Egypt.

Deuteronomy 20:1

The following men did not have to go to war:
1. A man who had not dedicated his new house
2. A man who had planted a new vineyard
3. A man engaged to marry
4. A man who was too afraid to go to battle

Today's Reading: Deuteronomy 18–20

March

6

When thou comest into the standing corn of thy neighbour, then thou mayest pluck the ears with thine hand; but thou shalt not move a sickle unto thy neighbour's standing corn.

Deuteronomy 23:25

The Lord's plan is for no one to go hungry. We are to care for others the same way we would want to be treated if we were in their predicament.

Today's Reading: Deuteronomy 21–23

7

Then thou shalt say before the LORD thy God, I have brought away the hallowed things out of mine house, and also have given them unto the Levite, and unto the stranger, to the fatherless, and to the widow, according to all thy commandments which thou hast commanded me: I have not transgressed thy commandments, neither have I forgotten them:

Deuteronomy 26:13

God expects us to care for those in need.

Today's Reading: Deuteronomy 24–26

March

8

And Moses and the priests the Levites spake unto all Israel, saying, Take heed, and hearken, O Israel; this day thou art become the people of the LORD thy God.

Deuteronomy 27:9

Have you been born again? Then thank God for it; if you haven't then don't wait another minute—make today your spiritual birthday.

Today's Reading: Deuteronomy 27–28

9

If any of thine be driven out unto the outmost parts of heaven, from thence will the LORD thy God gather thee, and from thence will he fetch thee:

Deuteronomy 30:4

God's desire is to bring us back into His fold no matter how far away we stray. If we truly repent in our hearts, then He is quick to forgive and accept us back into His ever-loving family.

Today's Reading: Deuteronomy 29–31

March

10

And there arose not a prophet since in Israel like unto Moses, whom the LORD knew face to face,

Deuteronomy 34:10

Beware of false prophets. The following are signs of a true prophet's message:
1. It will coincide with God's Word.
2. It will be clear.
3. It will be 100% accurate.

> Today's Reading: Deuteronomy 32–34

11

This book of the law shall not depart out of thy mouth; but thou shalt meditate therein day and night, that thou mayest observe to do according to all that is written therein: for then thou shalt make thy way prosperous, and then thou shalt have good success.

Joshua 1:8

Reading God's Word every morning and night is important, but it is also more important to do what the Word says.

> Today's Reading: Joshua 1–4

March

12

At that time the LORD said unto Joshua, Make thee sharp knives, and circumcise again the children of Israel the second time.

Joshua 5:2

Circumcision of a male's foreskin was a sign of God's covenant with Abraham. Today, circumcision of the male's foreskin is no longer mandatory; however, it is important to have a circumcised heart by loving and obeying God.

> Today's Reading: Joshua 5–7

13

And the princes said unto them, Let them live; but let them be hewers of wood and drawers of water unto all the congregation; as the princes had promised them.

Joshua 9:21

God expects us to search out diligently all things and to take nothing for granted. This helps to protect us from being double-crossed by others and having to go back on our promises.

> Today's Reading: Joshua 8–9

March

14

And all the spoil of these cities, and the cattle, the children of Israel took for a prey unto themselves; but every man they smote with the edge of the sword, until they had destroyed them, neither left they any to breathe.

Joshua 11:14

God delivered the Israelites from the large armies that came out to destroy them. Likewise, trust in God to deliver you from your enemies.

Today's Reading: Joshua 10–11

15

Then the children of Judah came unto Joshua in Gilgal: and Caleb the son of Jephunneh the Kenezite said unto him, Thou knowest the thing that the LORD said unto Moses the man of God concerning me and thee in Kadesh-barnea.

Joshua 14:6

Joshua and Caleb were the only spies that gave an honest report of the land of Canaan; they were also the only survivors allowed to enter Canaan. Liars cannot expect to receive God's blessings for doing dishonest work.

Today's Reading Joshua 12–14

March

16

And the children of Joseph said, The hill is not enough for us: and all the Canaanites that dwell in the land of the valley have chariots of iron, both they who are of Bethshean and her towns, and they who are of the valley of Jezreel.

Joshua 17:16

The Israelites were unable to capture the entire land promised to them because of their lack of faith and sin. As a result, today we still have wars and skirmishes in the Middle East.

> Today's Reading: Joshua 15–17

17

And the lot of the tribe of the children of Benjamin came up according to their families: and the coast of their lot came forth between the children of Judah and the children of Joseph.

Joshua 18:11

Benjamin is the only tribe that remained true to Judah when Jeroboam led the other ten tribes into rebellion. Although the tribe did not inherit large tracts of land, it did receive many important cities, including Jericho and parts of Jerusalem. Thus, God is always fair to the faithful.

> Today's Reading: Joshua 18–20

March

18

But take diligent heed to do the commandment and the law, which Moses the servant of the LORD charged you, to love the LORD your God, and to walk in all his ways, and to keep his commandments, and to cleave unto him, and to serve him with all your heart and with all your soul.

Joshua 22:5

We must be diligent in doing the work of our Father and not let the cares of this world interfere with our mission.

Today's Reading: Joshua 21–22

19

And I took your father Abraham from the other side of the flood, and led him throughout all the land of Canaan, and multiplied his seed, and gave him Isaac.

Joshua 24:3

What a day that will be, when God's only son, Jesus, takes us to the other side of Jordan and brings us home to be with Him.

Today's Reading: Joshua 23–24

March

20

And the children of Israel did evil in the sight of the LORD, and forgat the LORD their God, and served Baalim and the groves.

Judges 3:7

A person can be so mired down in sin he simply forgets whom God really is. Remember, if you are not serving the Lord, then you are serving the Devil and the self-righteous world.

Today's Reading: Judges 1–3

21

And she sent and called Barak the son of Abinoam out of Kedesh-naphtali, and said unto him, Hath not the LORD God of Israel commanded, saying, Go and draw toward mount Tabor, and take with thee ten thousand men of the children of Naphtali and of the children of Zebulun?

Judges 4:6

God sometimes uses women for prophecy, but they must not go against His teaching, and they must be 100% accurate as any other prophet of God must be.

Today's Reading: Judges 4–6

March

22

God hath delivered into your hands the princes of Midian, Oreb and Zeeb: and what was I able to do in comparison of you? Then their anger was abated toward him, when he had said that.

Judges 8:3

Gideon let the men of Ephraim know God had a greater plan for Ephraim than He did for Gideon's army. Remember, all work that is done to further the kingdom of God is important.

Today's Reading: Judges 7–8

23

And all the evil of the men of Shechem did God render upon their heads: and upon them came the curse of Jotham the son of Jerubbaal.

Judges 9:57

Abimelech unjustly murdered all 70 of his brothers, except for Jotham who escaped. In the end, God—being a just God—rendered to Abimelech and his men the justice they deserved.

Today's Reading: Judges 9–10

March

24

And the woman bare a son, and called his name Samson: and the child grew, and the LORD blessed him. And the Spirit of the LORD began to move him at times in the camp of Dan between Zorah and Eshtaol.

Judges 13:24-25

Samson, who was blessed with great strength, used most of his strength foolishly. He is a prime example of how people can waste their spiritual gifts for selfish indulgences.

Today's Reading: Judges 11–13

25

Then went Samson to Gaza, and saw there an harlot, and went in unto her.

Judges 16:1

A Nazarene was a person who dedicated his life to the Lord by avoiding such things as grape products (including wine), touching dead bodies, or shaving his hair. Although Samson may have appeared Godly on the outside, he was corrupt on the inside.

Today's Reading: Judges 14–16

March

26

And the man Micah had an house of gods, and made an ephod, and teraphim, and consecrated one of his sons, who became his priest. In those days there was no king in Israel, but every man did that which was right in his own eyes.
Judges 17:5-6

The problem is the same today as it was during the time of the judges. The lack of religion was not the problem—not *believing* in the true God was the problem.

Today's Reading: Judges 17–19

27

And said, O LORD God of Israel, why is this come to pass in Israel, that there should be to day one tribe lacking in Israel?
Judges 21:3

The tribe of Benjamin had become so rebellious they turned to raping and murdering innocent people. Because of this, God used the other eleven tribes to chastise the tribe of Benjamin. Even today, God uses other nations to punish wicked nations.

Today's Reading: Judges 20–21

March

28

And Ruth said, Intreat me not to leave thee, or to return from following after thee: for whither thou goest, I will go; and where thou lodgest, I will lodge: thy people shall be my people, and thy God my God:

Ruth 1:16

We must be like Naomi and tell others about God and the *Good News* of His son, Jesus Christ, who died for us.

Today's Reading: Ruth 1–4

29

She said unto her husband, I will not go up until the child be weaned, and then I will bring him, that he may appear before the LORD, and there abide for ever.

I Samuel 1:22

It is vital that we teach our children—the sooner the better—about the Lord. Not only must we teach them the scriptures each day, but our lives must also mirror our faith in God.

Today's Reading: I Samuel 1–3

March

30

And the men that died not were smitten with the emerods: and the cry of the city went up to heaven.

I Samuel 5:12

God smote the Philistines with emerods (hemorrhoids) in their secret parts because they treated the Ark of God as if it were mere booty.

> Today's Reading: I Samuel 4–7

31

Then said Saul to his servant, But, behold, if we go, what shall we bring the man? for the bread is spent in our vessels, and there is not a present to bring to the man of God: what have we?

I Samuel 9:7

Even during the times of the Old Testament it was customary to pay a minister for his services.

> Today's Reading: I Samuel 8–10

APRIL

1

And when they forgat the LORD their God, he sold them into the hand of Sisera, captain of the host of Hazor, and into the hand of the Philistines, and into the hand of the king of Moab, and they fought against them.
I Samuel 12:9

The Israelites wanted to be like the other nations and have an earthly king ruling over them instead of God. After God granted them their wish, they forsook Him and the curses increased.

Today's Reading: I Samuel 11–13

April

2

And Samuel said, Hath the LORD as great delight in burnt offerings and sacrifices, as in obeying the voice of the LORD? Behold, to obey is better than sacrifice, and to hearken than the fat of rams.

I Samuel 15:22

God owns everything, so we cannot out give God. However, God is more interested in our being obedient to Him rather than in our sacrifices to Him.

> Today's Reading: I Samuel 14–15

3

And it came to pass, when the evil spirit from God was upon Saul, that David took an harp, and played with his hand: so Saul was refreshed, and was well, and the evil spirit departed from him.

I Samuel 16:23

Praise and worship music to God might not only refresh a person, but it also might drive away evil spirits.

> Today's Reading: I Samuel 16–17

April

4

And Saul was afraid of David, because the LORD was with him, and was departed from Saul.
I Samuel 18:12

It is important that we remain in God's good graces to avoid His wrath.

> Today's Reading: I Samuel 18–20

5

And the king said to Doeg, Turn thou, and fall upon the priests. And Doeg the Edomite turned, and he fell upon the priests, and slew on that day fourscore and five persons that did wear a linen ephod.
I Samuel 22:18

Saul ordered his men to kill the 85 priests who had aided David—a man after God's own heart. Today, Christians around the world are slain because of their love for God.

> Today's Reading: I Samuel 21–24

April

6

For in very deed, as the LORD God of Israel liveth, which hath kept me back from hurting thee, except thou hadst hasted and come to meet me, surely there had not been left unto Nabal by the morning light any that pisseth against the wall.
I Samuel 25:34

Nabal offended David by not providing food for David's men who had been protecting Nabal's shepherds. Had Nabal's wife not brought the peace offering to David, Nabal and his men would have died.

Today's Reading: I Samuel 25–27

7

And Achish said unto the princes of the Philistines, Is not this David, the servant of Saul the king of Israel, which hath been with me these days, or these years, and I have found no fault in him since he fell unto me unto this day?
I Samuel 29:3

It is so important that we do good works so that others will stand by our reputation.

Today's Reading: I Samuel 28–31

April

8

And David said unto him, How went the matter? I pray thee, tell me. And he answered, That the people are fled from the battle, and many of the people also are fallen and dead; and Saul and Jonathan his son are dead also.

II Samuel 1:4

David loved Jonathan like a brother. He even loved Saul, his father-in-law, even though Saul tried several times to kill him. We must also pray for those who wish to cause us harm.

> Today's Reading: II Samuel 1–3

9

And Jonathan, Saul's son, had a son that was lame of his feet. He was five years old when the tidings came of Saul and Jonathan out of Jezreel, and his nurse took him up, and fled: and it came to pass, as she made haste to flee, that he fell, and became lame. And his name was Mephibosheth.

II Samuel 4:4

Thank God for nurses and other healthcare workers that care for us and our loved ones when we are ill.

> Today's Reading: II Samuel 4–7

April

10

And when the Syrians of Damascus came to succour Hadadezer king of Zobah, David slew of the Syrians two and twenty thousand men.
II Samuel 8:5

It is a sad fact that Syria and Israel remain bitter enemies even today. Pray that God will bring peace between these two nations, and that all Muslims and Jews will accept Jesus as their Lord and Savior.

Today's Reading: II Samuel 8–11

11

And he said, While the child was yet alive, I fasted and wept: for I said, Who can tell whether GOD will be gracious to me, that the child may live?
But now he is dead, wherefore should I fast? can I bring him back again? I shall go to him, but he shall not return to me.
II Samuel 12:22-23

God is a forgiving God, but sin always comes with a price. In David's case he lost his infant son because of his adultery with Bathsheba.

Today's Reading: II Samuel 12–13

April

12

So Absalom dwelt two full years in Jerusalem, and saw not the king's face.

II Samuel 14:28

Absalom was King David's son. David was upset with Absalom for murdering his own brother for raping their sister. Absalom would later rape David's concubines and try to take the kingdom from David by murdering him. Remember to pray each day for your family members.

> **Today's Reading: II Samuel 14–15**

13

They brought beds, and basons, and earthen vessels, and wheat, and barley, and flour, and parched corn, and beans, and lentiles, and parched pulse, and honey, and butter, and sheep, and cheese of kine, for David, and for the people that were with him, to eat: for they said, The people is hungry, and weary, and thirsty, in the wilderness.

II Samuel 17:28-29

We as a nation must pray each day for other nations and help them to know the Lord.

> **Today's Reading: II Samuel 16–17**

April

14

And Absalom rode upon a mule, and the mule went under the thick boughs of a great oak, and his head caught hold of the oak, and he was taken up between the heaven and the earth; and the mule that was under him went away.
II Samuel 18:9

Death is imminent for all of us and tragedy often strikes when we least expect it. As a result, we must be sure of our own salvation and of those we love.

Today's Reading: II Samuel 18–19

15

"...thou also hast lifted me up on high above them that rose up against me: thou hast delivered me from the violent man. Therefore I will give thanks unto thee, O LORD, among the heathen, and I will sing praises unto thy name".
II Samuel 22:49-50

Praise God for delivering you from your enemies that hate you for doing good. In addition, pray for your enemies that God will deliver them from a life of sin.

Today's Reading: II Samuel 20–22

April

16

The God of Israel said, the Rock of Israel spake to me, He that ruleth over men must be just, ruling in the fear of God. And he shall be as the light of the morning, when the sun riseth, even a morning without clouds; as the tender grass springing out of the earth by clear shining after rain.
II Samuel 23:3-4

Pray for unsaved judges that they will become born again. In addition, pray that all judges be just and unbiased when rendering their decisions and sentences.

> Today's Reading: II Samuel 23–24

17

Wherefore Nathan spake unto Bathsheba the mother of Solomon, saying, Hast thou not heard that Adonijah the son of Haggith doth reign, and David our lord knoweth it not? Now therefore come, let me, I pray thee, give thee counsel, that thou mayest save thine own life, and the life of thy son Solomon.
I Kings 1:11-12

Seek counselors that are Christians first in their lives and counselors second.

> Today's Reading: I Kings 1

April

18

And keep the charge of the LORD thy God, to walk in his ways, to keep his statutes, and his commandments, and his judgments, and his testimonies, as it is written in the law of Moses, that thou mayest prosper in all that thou doest, and whithersoever thou turnest thyself:

I Kings 2:3

To receive blessings from God, you must turn to Him and obey His commands.

Today's Reading: I Kings 2–3

19

Thou knowest how that David my father could not build an house unto the name of the LORD his God for the wars which were about him on every side, until the LORD put them under the soles of his feet.

I Kings 5:3

Our churches must be strong in the Lord to ward off the attacks of the Devil, who loves to shut down God's churches.

Today's Reading: I Kings 4–6

April

20

But Solomon was building his own house thirteen years, and he finished all his house.

I Kings 7:1

No other house can compare to the grand house that Solomon built. Nevertheless, we should be more concerned about the welfare of our own families that live in our *homes* rather than in our houses.

Today's Reading: I Kings 7

21

"When heaven is shut up, and there is no rain, because they have sinned against thee; if they pray toward this place, and confess thy name, and turn from their sin, when thou afflictest them: Then hear thou in heaven, and forgive the sin of thy servants, and of thy people Israel, that thou teach them the good way wherein they should walk, and give rain upon thy land, which thou hast given to thy people for an inheritance.

I Kings 8:35-36

Rain and bountiful harvests are gifts from God.

Today's Reading: I Kings 8

April

22

And all the people that were left of the Amorites, Hittites, Perizzites, Hivites, and Jebusites, which were not of the children of Israel, Their children that were left after them in the land, whom the children of Israel also were not able utterly to destroy, upon those did Solomon levy a tribute of bondservice unto this day.

I Kings 9:20-21

Individuals that do not follow the ways of God become slaves to Satan.

Today's Reading: I Kings 9–10

23

Whereupon the king took counsel, and made two calves of gold, and said unto them, It is too much for you to go up to Jerusalem: behold thy gods, O Israel, which brought thee up out of the land of Egypt.

I Kings 12:28

Jeroboam set up his own religion complete with idols, offerings, and priests, which went against God and His commandments. Individuals need to avoid people like Jeroboam and avoid all pseudo-Christian cults; they appear to have Christlike character on the outside, but inside they are demonic in nature.

Today's Reading: I Kings 11–12

April

24

He said unto him, I am a prophet also as thou art; and an angel spake unto me by the word of the LORD, saying, Bring him back with thee into thine house, that he may eat bread and drink water. But he lied unto him.

I Kings 13:18

Be careful of those who claim to have the gift of prophecy. Many false prophets have damaged God's churches and people.

> Today's Reading: I Kings 13–14

25

And Nadab the son of Jeroboam began to reign over Israel in the second year of Asa king of Judah, and reigned over Israel two years. And he did evil in the sight of the LORD, and walked in the way of his father, and in his sin wherewith he made Israel to sin.

I Kings 15:25-26

Christians should vote for Christian politicians that practice their faith in a Christ-like manner both in and out of the political arena.

> Today's Reading: I Kings 15–17

April

26

"...and I will dress the other bullock, and lay it on wood, and put no fire under: And call ye on the name of your gods, and I will call on the name of the LORD: and the God that answereth by fire, let him be God. And all the people answered and said, It is well spoken.

I Kings 18:23-24

Elijah knew that with God nothing is impossible. Likewise, God can supply all of our needs no matter how great or small they are.

Today's Reading: I Kings 18–19

27

And it came to pass, when Jezebel heard that Naboth was stoned, and was dead, that Jezebel said to Ahab, Arise, take possession of the vineyard of Naboth the Jezreelite, which he refused to give thee for money: for Naboth is not alive, but dead.

I Kings 21:15

The spilled blood of the innocent cries out to God, and He will judge—eventually—all murderers.

Today's Reading: I Kings 20–22

April

28

And they answered him, He was an hairy man, and girt with a girdle of leather about his loins. And he said, It is Elijah the Tishbite.

II Kings 1:8

God is not looking for men and women to bring a fashion statement to the lost; he is looking for those who have a passion to bring the lost to Him.

> Today's Reading: II Kings 1–2

29

And Elisha said unto her, What shall I do for thee? tell me, what hast thou in the house? And she said, Thine handmaid hath not any thing in the house, save a pot of oil. Then he said, Go, borrow thee vessels abroad of all thy neighbours, even empty vessels; borrow not a few.

II Kings 4:2-3

Everything needed to grow God's church is already available. We just need to tap into our resources and use them.

> Today's Reading: II Kings 3–4

April

30

"...and they said one to another, Lo, the king of Israel hath hired against us the kings of the Hittites, and the kings of the Egyptians, to come upon us. Wherefore they arose and fled in the twilight, and left their tents, and their horses, and their asses, even the camp as it was, and fled for their life.
II Kings 7:6-7

God can also bring fear upon our enemies—no matter how strong they might be—and cause them to flee from us.

Today's Reading: II Kings 5–7

MAY

1

And he said, Throw her down. So they threw her down: and some of her blood was sprinkled on the wall, and on the horses: and he trode her under foot. And when he was come in, he did eat and drink, and said, Go, see now this cursed woman, and bury her: for she is a king's daughter.
II Kings 9:33-34

Elijah prophesied wicked Jezebel would die and then dogs would eat her body; that is exactly what happened to her.

Today's Reading: II Kings 8–9

May

2

And the guard stood, every man with his weapons in his hand, round about the king, from the right corner of the temple to the left corner of the temple, along by the altar and the temple.

II Kings 11:11

Joash's own grandmother tried to murder him when he was an infant; at the age of seven he became a king. There is always a reason why God allows someone to become a ruler.

> Today's Reading: II Kings 10–12

3

"...wherein the LORD commanded, saying, The fathers shall not be put to death for the children, nor the children be put to death for the fathers; but every man shall be put to death for his own sin.

II Kings 14:5-6

We can pick our friends, but not our relatives. Therefore, we should not judge others based upon—good or bad—the reputations of their relatives.

> Today's Reading: II Kings 13–14

May

4

And Urijah the priest built an altar according to all that king Ahaz had sent from Damascus..."

II Kings 16:11

Ahaz was a corrupt king that sacrificed his son by fire to a strange god, and Urijah was a corrupt priest. Beware of leaders that shun God.

Today's Reading: II Kings 15–16

5

And the statutes, and the ordinances, and the law, and the commandment, which he wrote for you, ye shall observe to do for evermore; and ye shall not fear other gods.

II Kings 17:37

Fear in this case means to love. Our love should be to God and to no other god or gods.

Today's Reading: II Kings 17–18

May

6

Moreover Manasseh shed innocent blood very much, till he had filled Jerusalem from one end to another; beside his sin wherewith he made Judah to sin, in doing that which was evil in the sight of the LORD.

II Kings 21:16

Amon's officials murdered him two years after he became the king because he was evil like his father—Manasseh. Parents, be careful of the example you are setting for your own children to follow.

> Today's Reading: II Kings 19–21

7

Evilmerodach king of Babylon in the year that he began to reign did lift up the head of Jehoiachin king of Judah out of prison; And he spake kindly to him, and set his throne above the throne of the kings that were with him in Babylon; And changed his prison garments: and he did eat bread continually before him all the days of his life.

II Kings 25:27-29

Pray that the Lord will grant you peace and hope as you face trials and tribulations.

> Today's Reading: II Kings 22–25

May

8

And unto Eber were born two sons: the name of the one was Peleg; because in his days the earth was divided: and his brother's name was Joktan.

I Chronicles 1:19

The people built a tower in a city that would reach to heaven instead of spreading out. Therefore, God confused their language at the Tower of Babel and the people finally dispersed.

Today's Reading: I Chronicles 1

9

And when Azubah was dead, Caleb took unto him Ephrath, which bare him Hur.

I Chronicles 2:19

Genealogies were important to the Israelites because they wanted to be able to trace their heritage to Abraham. Similarly, Christians adopted into the family of God can trace their heritage to God the Father.

Today's Reading: I Chronicles 2–4

May

10

And the God of Israel stirred up the spirit of Pul king of Assyria, and the spirit of Tilgath-pilneser king of Assyria, and he carried them away, even the Reubenites, and the Gadites, and the half tribe of Manasseh, and brought them unto Halah, and Habor, and Hara, and to the river Gozan, unto this day.
I Chronicles 5:26

Be careful of what others around you believe, and do not be deceived by their false doctrines.

Today's Reading: : I Chronicles 5–6

11

So all Israel were reckoned by genealogies; and, behold, they were written in the book of the kings of Israel and Judah, who were carried away to Babylon for their transgression.
I Chronicles 9:1

Because of their transgressions, the people of Judah spent 70 years in captivity in Babylon as prophesied by Jeremiah and other prophets. After the 70 years ended, they returned to Jerusalem to rebuild Solomon's Temple.

Today's Reading: I Chronicles 7–9

May

12

"...the spirit came upon Amasai, who was chief of the captains, and he said, Thine are we, David, and on thy side, thou son of Jesse: peace, peace be unto thee, and peace be to thine helpers; for thy God helpeth thee".

I Chronicles 12:18

The Holy Spirit is our helper; Jesus said the Holy Spirit will guide us into all truth and will show us things yet to come (John 16:13, the author's paraphrase).

Today's Reading: I Chronicles 10–12

13

So David brought not the ark home to himself to the city of David, but carried it aside into the house of Obededom the Gittite.

I Chronicles 13:13

Steps to consider before making a major decision:
1. Study similar situations in the Bible
2. Pray about the matter
3. Seek godly counseling
4. Fast if you feel the need to
5. Trust God to help you through the situation

Today's Reading: I Chronicles 13–16

May

14

For I have not dwelt in an house since the day that I brought up Israel unto this day; but have gone from tent to tent, and from one tabernacle to another.
I Chronicles 17:5

Does God dwell in your heart? Our bodies are temples of God; therefore, we should respect not only our own bodies, but the bodies of others as well.

Today's Reading: I Chronicles 17–19

15

Now, my son, the LORD be with thee; and prosper thou, and build the house of the LORD thy God, as he hath said of thee.
I Chronicles 22:11

King David desired to build the Temple, but God would not allow it since David had shed so much blood. Instead, he allowed Solomon, David's son, to build the Temple. In other words David prepared, but Solomon built it.

Today's Reading: I Chronicles 20–23

May

16

Out of the spoils won in battles did they dedicate to maintain the house of the LORD.
I Chronicles 26:27

To show gratitude toward God for giving them victory over their enemies, the Israelites dedicated part of the spoils of war toward maintaining the Temple.

> **Today's Reading: I Chronicles 24–26**

17

And he died in a good old age, full of days, riches, and honour: and Solomon his son reigned in his stead.
I Chronicles 29:28

David was a man after God's own heart. As a result, God blessed David with a long, wealthy, prosperous, and honorable life. Therefore, David gave God the glory for all of these things. We must also remember to thank God for all of the blessings He has given to us.

> **Today's Reading: I Chronicles 27–29**

May

18

And, behold, I will give to thy servants, the hewers that cut timber, twenty thousand measures of beaten wheat, and twenty thousand measures of barley, and twenty thousand baths of wine, and twenty thousand baths of oil.
II Chronicles 2:10

It would cost over $1.5 TRILLION—not million or billion—to build Solomon's Temple in today's economy.

Today's Reading: II Chronicles 1–4

19

Have respect therefore to the prayer of thy servant, and to his supplication, O LORD my God, to hearken unto the cry and the prayer which thy servant prayeth before thee:
II Chronicles 6:19

It is interesting that King Solomon compares himself to a servant. In addition, Jesus Christ also referred to himself as a servant. As a result, Christians are also to be servants of the Most High God.

Today's Reading: II Chronicles 5–7

May

20

And the king answered them roughly; and king Rehoboam forsook the counsel of the old men, And answered them after the advice of the young men, saying, My father made your yoke heavy, but I will add thereto: my father chastised you with whips, but I will chastise you with scorpions.

II Chronicles 10:13-14

Wise elderly Christians are often one of the best resources to go to for advice.

Today's Reading: II Chronicles 8–10

21

So Abijah slept with his fathers, and they buried him in the city of David: and Asa his son reigned in his stead. In his days the land was quiet ten years.

II Chronicles 14:1

At the end of this ten-year period an Ethiopian king attacked King Asa of Judah with an army of 1 million soldiers—nearly double the size of King Asa's army. As a result, King Asa faithfully called upon God, and God easily destroyed the vast Ethiopian forces.

Today's Reading: II Chronicles 11–14

May

22

And they buried him in his own sepulchres, which he had made for himself in the city of David, and laid him in the bed which was filled with sweet odours and divers kinds of spices prepared by the apothecaries' art: and they made a very great burning for him.

II Chronicles 16:14

Unless the rapture occurs first, a man will certainly die the first death. Is your soul prepared for the afterlife?

Today's Reading: II Chronicles 15–18

23

And the destruction of Ahaziah was of God by coming to Joram: for when he was come, he went out with Jehoram against Jehu the son of Nimshi, whom the LORD had anointed to cut off the house of Ahab.

II Chronicles 22:7

Pray that God would give you victory over your enemies, no matter how powerful they may appear to be.

Today's Reading: II Chronicles 19–22

May

24

For the army of the Syrians came with a small company of men, and the LORD delivered a very great host into their hand, because they had forsaken the LORD God of their fathers. So they executed judgment against Joash.

II Chronicles 24:24

Joash abandoned the Lord after his godly mentor died, then killed his mentor's son. After the Syrian invasion, Joash's servants slew him while he was ill with disease. Never abandon God and always seek His blessings.

Today's Reading: II Chronicles 23–25

25

And now ye purpose to keep under the children of Judah and Jerusalem for bondmen and bondwomen unto you: but are there not with you, even with you, sins against the LORD your God?

II Chronicles 28:10

The prophet Oded reminded Israel they were also sinners and ordered Israel to release their captured brothers and sisters from Judah. We must be careful to remember our own sins before casting judgment upon others.

Today's Reading: II Chronicles 26–28

May

26

And said unto them, Hear me, ye Levites, sanctify now yourselves, and sanctify the house of the LORD God of your fathers, and carry forth the filthiness out of the holy place.
II Chronicles 29:5

King Hezekiah knew that in order to turn things around in his country the house of God had to be put in order first. Likewise, nations can only be truly successful when God's people and His churches are sanctified.

> Today's Reading: II Chronicles 29–30

27

For he built again the high places which Hezekiah his father had broken down, and he reared up altars for Baalim, and made groves, and worshipped all the host of heaven, and served them.
II Chronicles 33:3

King Manasseh built high towers in order to practice astrology. Thus, God had him carried off to Babylon where he repented of his sin and later returned to his throne in Jerusalem. God hates astrology because it is the work of the Devil.

> Today's Reading: II Chronicles 31–33

May

28

Jehoahaz was twenty and three years old when he began to reign, and he reigned three months in Jerusalem.
II Chronicles 36:2

The last four kings of Judah all turned their backs on God. Thus, Judah was invaded, its people taken captive, and they were exiled to foreign lands. God's prophets had warned them, but they still refused to obey. As a result, they spent 70 years in captivity in Babylon.

Today's Reading: II Chronicles 34–36

29

Who is there among you of all his people? His God be with him, and let him go up to Jerusalem, which is in Judah, and build the house of the LORD God of Israel (he is the God), which is in Jerusalem.
Ezra 1:3

God's desire is that we continue to build the house of the Lord. We do this by leading others to the saving grace of Jesus Christ.

Today's Reading: Ezra 1–2

May

30

Then the people of the land weakened the hands of the people of Judah, and troubled them in building, And hired counsellors against them, to frustrate their purpose, all the days of Cyrus king of Persia, even until the reign of Darius king of Persia.

Ezra 4:4-5

Anytime God's people set out to do something great for the Lord, those that are against the Lord will oppose them.

Today's Reading: Ezra 3–5

31

For Ezra had prepared his heart to seek the law of the LORD, and to do it, and to teach in Israel statutes and judgments.

Ezra 7:10

It is important to attend church as often as possible. For it is through the anointed preaching and teaching of the church that we learn about God and His ways.

Today's Reading: Ezra 6–8

JUNE

1

Now therefore let us make a covenant with our God to put away all the wives, and such as are born of them, according to the counsel of my lord, and of those that tremble at the commandment of our God; and let it be done according to the law.

Ezra 10:3

God hates divorce, but in this case their foreign wives were practicing idolatry and fornication, thus God demanded the men to divorce their wives in order to remain faithful to Him.

Today's Reading: Ezra 9–10

June

2

Now these are thy servants and thy people, whom thou hast redeemed by thy great power, and by thy strong hand.

Nehemiah 1:10

God's strong hand redeems us. This same hand can crush an army in an instant and gently wipe away the tears of His children.

> **Today's Reading: Nehemiah 1–3**

3

And I sent messengers unto them, saying, I am doing a great work, so that I cannot come down: why should the work cease, whilst I leave it, and come down to you?

Nehemiah 6:3

When God calls you to do something great on His behalf, don't let Satan rob you of your mission. Instead, be strong in the Lord.

> **Today's Reading: Nehemiah 4–6**

June

4

Also day by day, from the first day unto the last day, he read in the book of the law of God. And they kept the feast seven days; and on the eighth day was a solemn assembly, according unto the manner.

Nehemiah 8:18

The people held an eight-day celebration to thank God for allowing the wall around the city to be rebuilt. We should also remember to thank God for what he is doing in our lives.

> Today's Reading: Nehemiah 7–8

5

And shewedst signs and wonders upon Pharaoh, and on all his servants, and on all the people of his land: for thou knewest that they dealt proudly against them. So didst thou get thee a name, as it is this day.

Nehemiah 9:10

Jesus promised He would *never* leave us nor forsake us.

> Today's Reading: Nehemiah 9–10

June

6

Thus cleansed I them from all strangers, and appointed the wards of the priests and the Levites, every one in his business; And for the wood offering, at times appointed, and for the firstfruits. Remember me, O my God, for good.
Nehemiah 13:30–31

Nehemiah turned his people toward God. How do you want God to remember you? Are you living an obedient life that is pleasing to Him?

Today's Reading: Nehemiah 11–13

7

And he brought up Hadassah, that is, Esther, his uncle's daughter: for she had neither father nor mother, and the maid was fair and beautiful; whom Mordecai, when her father and mother were dead, took for his own daughter.
Esther 2:7

It is important for families to stay together, if possible. As children of God, God adopts us into His family and becomes our Father.

Today's Reading: Esther 1–3

June

8

And the king said, Who is in the court? Now Haman was come into the outward court of the king's house, to speak unto the king to hang Mordecai on the gallows that he had prepared for him.

Esther 6:4

A man's pride will eventually bring him down, and sometimes it will cost him dearly. Therefore, learn to be humble.

Today's Reading: Esther 4–7

9

And Esther spake yet again before the king, and fell down at his feet, and besought him with tears to put away the mischief of Haman the Agagite, and his device that he had devised against the Jews.

Esther 8:3

When life seems unbearable follow the example of Esther, but instead of humbling yourself before a human king, humble yourself before the King of kings.

Today's Reading: Esther 8–10

June

10

They are destroyed from morning to evening: they perish for ever without any regarding it. Doth not their excellency which is in them go away? they die, even without wisdom.

Job 4:20-21

Job's friends came to comfort him, but instead they brought him more misery by telling Job that he brought all of his problems upon himself because of his sins. We are not to judge others, especially when they are suffering.

Today's Reading: Job 1–5

11

My brethren have dealt deceitfully as a brook, and as the stream of brooks they pass away;

Job 6:15

Get as much information as you can about a situation before passing judgment upon others. Not all things are as they seem.

Today's Reading: Job 6–10

June

12

For thou hast said, My doctrine is pure, and I am clean in thine eyes.

Job 11:4

Not all church doctrines are the same. Therefore, it is important to study God's Word to determine if what is in a doctrine is truly of God.

> Today's Reading: Job 11–15

13

He shall fly away as a dream, and shall not be found: yea, he shall be chased away as a vision of the night.

Job 20:8

Decades after a person dies, seldom are they remembered. On the other hand, if someone does something famous—or infamous—people tend to remember them—at least for awhile. How do you want people to remember you?

> Today's Reading: Job 16–21

June

14

And if it be not so now, who will make me a liar, and make my speech nothing worth?

Job 24:25

Job reminds us of the importance of always speaking the truth.

> **Today's Reading: Job 22–28**

15

His flesh shall be fresher than a child's: he shall return to the days of his youth.

Job 33:25

When the Lord calls His children home to heaven, He gives them new bodies that are no longer prone to sickness or disease.

> **Today's Reading: Job 29–33**

June

16

For truly my words shall not be false: he that is perfect in knowledge is with thee.

Job 36:4

In Jesus there was found no sin—not even a single lie.

> Today's Reading: Job 34–37

17

Canst thou draw out leviathan with an hook? or his tongue with a cord which thou lettest down?
Out of his mouth go burning lamps, and sparks of fire leap out. Out of his nostrils goeth smoke, as out of a seething pot or caldron.

Job 41:1, 19-20

Leviathan was possibly a fire-breathing dragon that became extinct.

> Today's Reading: Job 38–42

June

18

He made a pit, and digged it, and is fallen into the ditch which he made.

Psalms 7:15

Sometimes sin can get us into deep trouble, and God may be our only way out.

> Today's Reading: Psalms 1–9

19

But I have trusted in thy mercy; my heart shall rejoice in thy salvation.

Psalms 13:5

Christians know this world is not their home. They rejoice in knowing that their eternal home is with the Father. Therefore, set your mind on things above.

> Today's Reading: Psalms 10–17

June

20

The fear of the LORD is clean, enduring for ever: the judgments of the LORD are true and righteous altogether.
Psalms 19:9

To fear God is to love Him. If we obey His voice, then His judgments upon us will be a blessing to us.

> Today's Reading: Psalms 18–22

21

I will extol thee, O LORD; for thou hast lifted me up, and hast not made my foes to rejoice over me.
Psalms 30:1

Give thanks to God for making your enemies to be at peace with you and allowing them to become your friends.

> Today's Reading: Psalms 23–31

June

22

Let their way be dark and slippery: and let the angel of the LORD persecute them.

Psalms 35:6

When others try to persecute you, turn to God for your safety.

Today's Reading: Psalms 32–37

23

But thou hast saved us from our enemies, and hast put them to shame that hated us.

Psalms 44:7

When things seem hopeless, and the enemy is knocking at your door, put your faith in God and trust Him to deliver you from your situation.

Today's Reading: Psalms 38–44

June

24

There is a river, the streams whereof shall make glad the city of God, the holy place of the tabernacles of the most High. God is in the midst of her; she shall not be moved: God shall help her, and that right early.

Psalms 46:4-5

The mountains may shake and the seas may roar, but those who trust in the Lord shall abide in His safety.

Today's Reading: Psalms 45–51

25

Every one of them is gone back: they are altogether become filthy; there is none that doeth good, no, not one.

Psalms 53:3

Jesus tells us not to worry about the splinter in our neighbor's eye, but to worry about the log in our own eye (Matthew 7:5, the author's paraphrase).

Today's Reading: Psalms 52–59

June

26

The pastures are clothed with flocks; the valleys also are covered over with corn; they shout for joy, they also sing.

Psalms 65:13

God blesses the land when its people are obedient to Him.

> Today's Reading: Psalms 60–67

27

But I will hope continually, and will yet praise thee more and more.

Psalms 71:14

Praise God's holy name during the good times and the bad.

> Today's Reading: Psalms 68–71

June

28

Thou holdest mine eyes waking: I am so troubled that I cannot speak I have considered the days of old, the years of ancient times.

Psalms 77:4-5

When we are going through a difficult time, it seems like no one cares about our situation. The good news is God cares and understands, and things will get better if we turn them over to the Lord and put our trust in Him.

> **Today's Reading: Psalms 72–77**

29

Help us, O God of our salvation, for the glory of thy name: and deliver us, and purge away our sins, for thy name's sake.

Psalms 79:9

We all must come to the Lord before it is too late. Even prisoners on death row have the opportunity to come to Him before their time is up. Pray for those in prison and for prison chaplains.

> **Today's Reading: Psalms 78–81**

June

30

Surely his salvation is nigh them that fear him; that glory may dwell in our land.

Psalms 85:9

God will bless all nations whose people love and obey Him.

Today's Reading: Psalms 82–89

JULY

1

For the LORD will not cast off his people, neither will he forsake his inheritance.

Psalms 94:14

The Lord will remain faithful to His people, even if He has to punish them for being disobedient to Him.

Today's Reading: Psalms 90–97

July

2

Before the LORD; for he cometh to judge the earth: with righteousness shall he judge the world, and the people with equity.

Psalms 98:9

The judges on earth represent the divine judge. Therefore, they are to be unbiased in their decisions and not play favoritism over justice.

> **Today's Reading: Psalms 98–104**

3

O give thanks unto the LORD, for he is good: for his mercy endureth for ever. Let the redeemed of the LORD say so, whom he hath redeemed from the hand of the enemy;

Psalms 107:1-2

One way we can give thanks to the Lord is to go to church on a regular basis and lift up our voices to Him in praise and worship.

> **Today's Reading: Psalms 105–107**

July

4

Through God we shall do valiantly: for he it is that shall tread down our enemies.

Psalms 108:13

Pray that God will bring you courage to conquer your fears.

> Today's Reading: Psalms 108–112

5

O praise the LORD, all ye nations: praise him, all ye people.

Psalms 117:1

We are to be one nation under God.

> Today's Reading: Psalms 113–118

July

6

With my lips have I declared all the judgments of thy mouth.
Psalms 119:13

Do not jump to conclusions; things are not always the way they appear to be. In other words, be quick to listen and slow to speak.

Today's Reading: Psalms 119

7

Let Israel hope in the LORD from henceforth and for ever.
Psalms 131:3

Pray for your Jewish friends and tell them about Jesus and His love for them. Also, remember to pray for the nation of Israel and the neighboring countries that surround Israel.

Today's Reading: Psalms 120–135

July

8

I cried unto thee, O LORD: I said, Thou art my refuge and my portion in the land of the living.

Psalms 142:5

"They said unto them, Why seek ye the living among the dead? He is not here, but is risen" (Luke 24:5-6). Jesus continues to be our refuge in times of trouble, and He continues to supply our every need.

Today's Reading: Psalms 136–142

9

Which executeth judgment for the oppressed: which giveth food to the hungry. The LORD looseth the prisoners:

Psalms 146:7

Pray for those falsely imprisoned, beaten, and tortured for loving Jesus. Also, remember their families that God will bring them comfort, strength, and peace.

Today's Reading: Psalms 143–150

July

10

The curse of the LORD is in the house of the wicked: but he blesseth the habitation of the just.

Proverbs 3:33

Our homes should be a reflection of what heaven is all about. It should be filled with peace, love, and joy—not bitterness, envy, and strife.

> **Today's Reading: Proverbs 1–4**

11

Drink waters out of thine own cistern, and running waters out of thine own well.

Proverbs 5:15

Unfortunately, nearly half of all marriages in the United States, both Christian and non-Christian, end in divorce within eight years.

> **Today's Reading: Proverbs 5–8**

July

12

There is that maketh himself rich, yet hath nothing: there is that maketh himself poor, yet hath great riches.
Proverbs 13:7

True wealth is not measured by how much you own, but by the gifts God has given to you and what you do with those gifts.

> Today's Reading: Proverbs 9–13

13

A reproof entereth more into a wise man than an hundred stripes into a fool.
Proverbs 17:10

A wise person will be thankful to a person that points out his mistakes, but a fool will hate those who correct him.

> Today's Reading: Proverbs 14–17

July

14

There are many devices in a man's heart; nevertheless the counsel of the LORD, that shall stand.
Proverbs 19:21

When you are not sure which path in life to take, ask the Lord to be your guide; He will see you through.

> Today's Reading: Proverbs 18–21

15

Prepare thy work without, and make it fit for thyself in the field; and afterwards build thine house.
Proverbs 24:27

It is wise for a young person to get a good post-secondary education and learn a trade before marrying and settling down to raise a family.

> Today's Reading: Proverbs 22–24

July

16

For the transgression of a land many are the princes thereof: but by a man of understanding and knowledge the state thereof shall be prolonged.
                                                        Proverbs 28:2

Politicians that serve the greedy interests of themselves and other wicked people, bring shame and misery upon the land.

Today's Reading: Proverbs 25–28

17

Every word of God is pure: he is a shield unto them that put their trust in him. Add thou not unto his words, lest he reprove thee, and thou be found a liar.
                                                        Proverbs 30:5-6

Do not believe everything you hear about the Bible. Instead, read God's word for yourself and see if the saying is true.

Today's Reading: Proverbs 29–31

July

18

As he came forth of his mother's womb, naked shall he return to go as he came, and shall take nothing of his labour, which he may carry away in his hand.
Ecclesiastes 5:15

As a steward of God, you should leave either a notarized will or a trust to your loved ones before you die. This is something usually handled best by a trained and experienced trusts and estates lawyer.

> Today's Reading: Ecclesiastes 1–6

19

Let us hear the conclusion of the whole matter: Fear God, and keep his commandments: for this is the whole duty of man. For God shall bring every work into judgment, with every secret thing, whether it be good, or whether it be evil.
Ecclesiastes 12:13-14

We should be more concerned with storing up treasures in heaven, instead of here on earth, because we cannot take our earthly treasures with us when we die.

> Today's Reading: Ecclesiastes 7–12

July

20

A garden inclosed is my sister, my spouse; a spring shut up, a fountain sealed.

Song of Solomon 4:12

Solomon's bride to be is a virgin and not an adulterous woman. Likewise, we need to teach children to respect their bodies as an enclosed garden.

Today's Reading: Song of Solomon 1–8

21

And it shall come to pass, that he that is left in Zion, and he that remaineth in Jerusalem, shall be called holy, even every one that is written among the living in Jerusalem:

Isaiah 4:3

This passage refers to those who survive a judgment and have not turned away from God. They will be "holy" and have the character of the "Holy One of Israel."

Today's Reading: Isaiah 1–4

July

22

Also I heard the voice of the Lord, saying, Whom shall I send, and who will go for us? Then said I, Here am I; send me.

Isaiah 6:8

Jesus said that many are called but few are chosen when He referred to the call of salvation going out to so many people. Unfortunately, those who do respond to God's call, repent of their sins, and become adopted into the family of God are only a few of the many who are called.

Today's Reading: Isaiah 5–8

23

O Assyrian, the rod of mine anger, and the staff in their hand is mine indignation. I will send him against an hypocritical nation, and against the people of my wrath will I give him a charge, to take the spoil, and to take the prey, and to tread them down like the mire of the streets.

Isaiah 10:5-6

Pray for your nation that its citizens will seek the will of God and avoid His wrath.

Today's Reading: Isaiah 9–12

July

24

How art thou fallen from heaven, O Lucifer, son of the morning! how art thou cut down to the ground, which didst weaken the nations!

Isaiah 14:12

God created Satan as the most beautiful angel and filled him with wisdom, but because of his pride God threw him out of heaven. Do not let your pride keep you from heaven.

> **Today's Reading: Isaiah 13–16**

25

In the day shalt thou make thy plant to grow, and in the morning shalt thou make thy seed to flourish: but the harvest shall be a heap in the day of grief and of desperate sorrow.

Isaiah 17:11

Sometimes we try to do everything *humanly possible* to make things right, but our efforts are futile. Therefore, we must turn back to the *Rock of Our Salvation* to make things right again.

> **Today's Reading: Isaiah 17–21**

July

26

Is this your joyous city, whose antiquity is of ancient days? her own feet shall carry her afar off to sojourn.

Isaiah 23:7

Study the history of the city, or town, which is closest to where you live. Was it founded upon Godly principles? Check its charter and find out, and pray for your city or town.

> Today's Reading: Isaiah 22–25

27

And it shall come to pass in that day, that the great trumpet shall be blown, and they shall come which were ready to perish in the land of Assyria, and the outcasts in the land of Egypt, and shall worship the LORD in the holy mount at Jerusalem.

Isaiah 27:13

Pray for the leaders of other nations that their souls would be saved, and that they would become servants of Jesus Christ.

> Today's Reading: Isaiah 26–28

July

28

Surely your turning of things upside down shall be esteemed as the potter's clay: for shall the work say of him that made it, He made me not? or shall the thing framed say of him that framed it, He had no understanding?

Isaiah 29:16

God is the potter, and we are the clay.

Today's Reading: Isaiah 29–31

29

And an highway shall be there, and a way, and it shall be called The way of holiness; the unclean shall not pass over it; but it shall be for those: the wayfaring men, though fools, shall not err therein.

Isaiah 35:8

Are you ready to walk on the King's highway? Tell others about *"the Way, the Truth, and the Life"* (John 14:6).

Today's Reading: Isaiah 32–35

July

30

The living, the living, he shall praise thee, as I do this day: the father to the children shall make known thy truth.

Isaiah 38:19

Does your family read the Bible and pray together every day? If your answer is "yes", that is wonderful! If not, then make it a daily habit starting today.

> **Today's Reading: Isaiah 36–38**

31

I the LORD have called thee in righteousness, and will hold thine hand, and will keep thee, and give thee for a covenant of the people, for a light of the Gentiles; To open the blind eyes, to bring out the prisoners from the prison, and them that sit in darkness out of the prison house.

Isaiah 42:6-7

God is calling believers to bring His light to those that are spiritually blind, so that they may be free from spiritual darkness.

> **Today's Reading: Isaiah 39–42**

AUGUST

1

I have not spoken in secret, in a dark place of the earth: I said not unto the seed of Jacob, Seek ye me in vain: I the LORD speak righteousness, I declare things that are right.
Isaiah 45:19

Study the Bible every day, so that you may live according to God's will.

Today's Reading: Isaiah 43–47

August

2

Thus saith the Lord GOD, Behold, I will lift up mine hand to the Gentiles, and set up my standard to the people: and they shall bring thy sons in their arms, and thy daughters shall be carried upon their shoulders.

Isaiah 49:22

God's promise was not just for the nation of Israel; Christ's suffering at the cross was for everyone's sin.

> Today's Reading: Isaiah 48–51

3

All we like sheep have gone astray; we have turned every one to his own way; and the LORD hath laid on him the iniquity of us all.

Isaiah 53:6

Jesus came to earth because of our sinful ways. Fortunately, for us, He gave his life so that we would not perish, but have eternal life.

> Today's Reading: Isaiah 52–56

August

4

For he put on righteousness as a breastplate, and an helmet of salvation upon his head; and he put on the garments of vengeance for clothing, and was clad with zeal as a cloke.

Isaiah 59:17

The Lord is just when he repays an unrepentant sinner with vengeance.

Today's Reading: Isaiah 57–59

5

I will greatly rejoice in the LORD, my soul shall be joyful in my God; for he hath clothed me with the garments of salvation, he hath covered me with the robe of righteousness, as a bridegroom decketh himself with ornaments, and as a bride adorneth herself with her jewels.

Isaiah 61:10

How beautiful are the spiritual clothes of those who have come to Christ.

Today's Reading: Isaiah 60–63

August

6

For, behold, the LORD will come with fire, and with his chariots like a whirlwind, to render his anger with fury, and his rebuke with flames of fire. For by fire and by his sword will the LORD plead with all flesh: and the slain of the LORD shall be many.

Isaiah 66:15-16

Believers in Christ are protected from the fires of Hell just like Shadrach, Meshach, and Abednego, who were thrown into a blazing furnace for not worshiping a statue (Daniel 3:16-18).

Today's Reading: Isaiah 64–66

7

For, behold, I have made thee this day a defenced city, and an iron pillar, and brasen walls against the whole land, against the kings of Judah, against the princes thereof, against the priests thereof, and against the people of the land. And they shall fight against thee; but they shall not prevail against thee; for I am with thee, saith the LORD, to deliver thee.

Jeremiah 1:18-19

When in doubt, put your trust in the Lord.

Today's Reading: Jeremiah 1–3

August

8

Be thou instructed, O Jerusalem, lest my soul depart from thee; lest I make thee desolate, a land not inhabited.
Jeremiah 6:8

There are ancient cities in the Middle East, such as Petra—a once prosperous town located on a trade route in Edom that once flourished but now lies in ruins because of its sins.

> **Today's Reading: Jeremiah 4–6**

9

Is there no balm in Gilead; is there no physician there? why then is not the health of the daughter of my people recovered?
Jeremiah 8:22

The best medicine in the world cannot heal some people because of their sin.

> **Today's Reading: Jeremiah 7–9**

August

10

O LORD, I know that the way of man is not in himself: it is not in man that walketh to direct his steps. O LORD, correct me, but with judgment; not in thine anger, lest thou bring me to nothing.

Jeremiah 10:23-24

Although others may not forgive you for the pain you have caused them, you must ask God to forgive you when you have wronged others.

Today's Reading: Jeremiah 10–12

11

What wilt thou say when he shall punish thee? for thou hast taught them to be captains, and as chief over thee: shall not sorrows take thee, as a woman in travail?

Jeremiah 13:21

Sin can bring such pain into our lives it hurts like a mother giving birth.

Today's Reading: Jeremiah 13–15

August

12

Blessed is the man that trusteth in the LORD, and whose hope the LORD is.

Jeremiah 17:7

Are you putting your hope and trust in the Lord?

Today's Reading: Jeremiah 16–18

13

Sing unto the LORD, praise ye the LORD: for he hath delivered the soul of the poor from the hand of evildoers.

Jeremiah 20:13

Sing praises to God for the blessings He has given you and for the blessings yet to come.

Today's Reading: Jeremiah 19–22

August

14

Behold, the days come, saith the LORD, that I will raise unto David a righteous Branch, and a King shall reign and prosper, and shall execute judgment and justice in the earth.

Jeremiah 23:5

Jesus Christ will fulfill this promise when He comes during the Second Coming.

> Today's Reading: Jeremiah 23–24

15

They shall be carried to Babylon, and there shall they be until the day that I visit them, saith the LORD; then will I bring them up, and restore them to this place.

Jeremiah 27:22

Just as there was hope for the Jews carried away to Babylon, there is also hope for innocent Christians cast into prison.

> Today's Reading: Jeremiah 25–27

August

16

Alas! for that day is great, so that none is like it: it is even the time of Jacob's trouble; but he shall be saved out of it.

Jeremiah 30:7

This verse points to a future time when a remnant of the Jewish people will remain faithful to God even though they will be persecuted during the Tribulation period. This persecution will end, however, when Christ returns to establish His kingdom on earth.

> **Today's Reading: Jeremiah 28–30**

17

For there shall be a day, that the watchmen upon the mount Ephraim shall cry, Arise ye, and let us go up to Zion unto the LORD our God.

Jeremiah 31:6

God commands His people to be watchmen and to wait for His return; He also tells His people to tell others the *Good News* of Jesus Christ.

> **Today's Reading: Jeremiah 31–32**

August

18

Thus saith the LORD of hosts, the God of Israel; Go and tell the men of Judah and the inhabitants of Jerusalem, Will ye not receive instruction to hearken to my words? saith the LORD.
Jeremiah 35:13

After Christ returns to earth, Jews from all over the world will return to Jerusalem and experience true peace and happiness.

> Today's Reading: Jeremiah 33–35

19

Moreover Jeremiah said unto king Zedekiah, What have I offended against thee, or against thy servants, or against this people, that ye have put me in prison? Where are now your prophets which prophesied unto you, saying, The king of Babylon shall not come against you, nor against this land?
Jeremiah 37:18-19

Beware of astrologers, palm readers, and other fortunetellers because fortune telling is satanic in nature, and God prohibits it.

> Today's Reading: Jeremiah 36–38

August

20

Then the king of Babylon slew the sons of Zedekiah in Riblah before his eyes: also the king of Babylon slew all the nobles of Judah. Moreover he put out Zedekiah's eyes, and bound him with chains, to carry him to Babylon.

Jeremiah 39:6-7

War is hell. Zedekiah should have listened to God's prophet instead of to the soothsayers.

Today's Reading: Jeremiah 39–41

21

But we will certainly do whatsoever thing goeth forth out of our own mouth, to burn incense unto the queen of heaven, and to pour out drink offerings unto her, as we have done, we, and our fathers, our kings, and our princes, in the cities of Judah, and in the streets of Jerusalem....

Jeremiah 44:17

Those that continue to follow the religions of the world and refuse the ways of God are ripe for God's judgment.

Today's Reading: Jeremiah 42–44

August

22

The word that the LORD spake to Jeremiah the prophet, how Nebuchadrezzar king of Babylon should come and smite the land of Egypt.

Jeremiah 46:13

Jeremiah tells Egypt that their army will be defeated because they put their trust in their large army and not in God. Big armies do not always win wars; God determines who wins wars.

> Today's Reading: Jeremiah 45–48

23

At the noise of the taking of Babylon the earth is moved, and the cry is heard among the nations.

Jeremiah 50:46

Stay tuned to what is happening in Iraq. This is where ancient Babylon is located and where the fulfillment of future biblical prophecies shall take place.

> Today's Reading: Jeremiah 49–50

August

24

Wherefore, behold, the days come, saith the LORD, that I will do judgment upon her graven images: and through all her land the wounded shall groan.
                                                    Jeremiah 51:52

God used Babylon to punish Israel for its idolatry. Later, He will punish Babylon for its idolatry. Thus, neither nation went unpunished for its idolatry. Today, God still uses other nations to punish other nations for their idolatry and other sins.

> **Today's Reading: Jeremiah 51–52**

25

All thine enemies have opened their mouth against thee: they hiss and gnash the teeth: they say, We have swallowed her up: certainly this is the day that we looked for; we have found, we have seen it.
                                                    Lamentations 2:16

Israel's enemies rejoiced over her downfall. Likewise, the United States' enemies would love to see her brought to her knees also. To prevent this from happening, we must pray for revival in America.

> **Today's Reading: Lamentations 1–2**

August

26

Turn thou us unto thee, O LORD, and we shall be turned; renew our days as of old.

Lamentations 5:21

America was founded upon biblical principles. If we are to flourish once again as a nation, then we must come back and embrace those very same principles once again.

> Today's Reading: Lamentations 3–5

27

And the living creatures ran and returned as the appearance of a flash of lightning.

Ezekiel 1:14

The rapid movements of the cherubim reminds us of the lightning speed of Christ when He shall return for his people.

> Today's Reading: Ezekiel 1–4

August

28

Also, thou son of man, thus saith the Lord GOD unto the land of Israel; An end, the end is come upon the four corners of the land.

Ezekiel 7:2

Israel fell, as foretold by Ezekiel, because of her sin. Since the Jewish people have openly rejected Jesus as their Lord and Savior, Israel will fall again.

Today's Reading: Ezekiel 5–8

29

And the LORD said unto him, Go through the midst of the city, through the midst of Jerusalem, and set a mark upon the foreheads of the men that sigh and that cry for all the abominations that be done in the midst thereof.

Ezekiel 9:4

Those with the mark on their foreheads were spared judgment. Likewise, those that belong to Christ will be spared eternity in hell.

Today's Reading: Ezekiel 9–12

August

30

Though these three men were in it, as I live, saith the Lord GOD, they shall deliver neither sons nor daughters, but they only shall be delivered themselves.

Ezekiel 14:18

Christians must be careful how they are raising their children. Influences by society can be enough to keep them from being saved.

Today's Reading: Ezekiel 13–15

31

And say, Thus saith the Lord GOD unto Jerusalem; Thy birth and thy nativity is of the land of Canaan; thy father was an Amorite, and thy mother an Hittite.

Ezekiel 16:3

The people of Israel were committing adultery with people from neighboring countries. As a result, God punished Israel for her sins.

Today's Reading: Ezekiel 16

SEPTEMBER

1

And he knew their desolate palaces, and he laid waste their cities; and the land was desolate, and the fulness thereof, by the noise of his roaring.

Ezekiel 19:7

God's strength is always mightier than any military fort, army, or weapon.

Today's Reading: Ezekiel 17–19

September

2

Thou therefore, son of man, prophesy, and smite thine hands together, and let the sword be doubled the third time, the sword of the slain: it is the sword of the great men that are slain, which entereth into their privy chambers.
Ezekiel 21:14

Israel was slaughtered because she refused to be disciplined by the Lord. We as a nation must always be true to God; otherwise, we will also pay the consequences for our sins.

Today's Reading: Ezekiel 20–21

3

Son of man, say unto her, Thou art the land that is not cleansed, nor rained upon in the day of indignation.
Ezekiel 22:24

Drought may be a sign that God is punishing the people who live in that region.

Today's Reading: Ezekiel 22–23

September

4

He shall slay with the sword thy daughters in the field: and he shall make a fort against thee, and cast a mount against thee, and lift up the buckler against thee.
                                                    Ezekiel 26:8

God also punished Tyre, Israel's neighbor, for showing no mercy over Israel's downfall.

Today's Reading: Ezekiel 24–26

5

The merchants among the people shall hiss at thee; thou shalt be a terror, and never shalt be any more.
                                                    Ezekiel 27:36

Tyre was a coastal nation known for her sea trading among many nations. However, her sin was so great that God sunk her ships, destroyed her ports, and destroyed the rest of her city.

Today's Reading: Ezekiel 27–28

September

6

Son of man, Nebuchadrezzar king of Babylon caused his army to serve a great service against Tyrus: every head was made bald, and every shoulder was peeled: yet had he no wages, nor his army, for Tyrus, for the service that he had served against it:

Ezekiel 29:18

Conquering armies often shaved off their war captives' hair and stripped them bare.

Today's Reading: Ezekiel 29–31

7

But if the watchman see the sword come, and blow not the trumpet, and the people be not warned; if the sword come, and take any person from among them, he is taken away in his iniquity; but his blood will I require at the watchman's hand.

Ezekiel 33:6

Believers are responsible to warn others of Christ's coming and their need for salvation.

Today's Reading: Ezekiel 32–33

September

8

Therefore thus saith the Lord GOD; Surely in the fire of my jealousy have I spoken against the residue of the heathen, and against all Idumea, which have appointed my land into their possession with the joy of all their heart, with despiteful minds, to cast it out for a prey.

Ezekiel 36:5

God will punish nations that try to take away the Promised Land from Israel.

Today's Reading: Ezekiel 34–36

9

Be thou prepared, and prepare for thyself, thou, and all thy company that are assembled unto thee, and be thou a guard unto them.

Ezekiel 38:7

In the last days armies will surround the nation of Israel, but God will give Israel victory over her enemies.

Today's Reading: Ezekiel 37–38

September

10

And ye shall eat fat till ye be full, and drink blood till ye be drunken, of my sacrifice which I have sacrificed for you.
                                                        Ezekiel 39:19

In the last great battle, birds and wild beasts will feast upon the remains of the soldiers that will try to invade Israel.

Today's Reading: Ezekiel 39–40

11

The altar of wood was three cubits high, and the length thereof two cubits; and the corners thereof, and the length thereof, and the walls thereof, were of wood: and he said unto me, This is the table that is before the LORD.
                                                        Ezekiel 41:22

During the millennium when Christ comes back to reign, Solomon's Temple will be rebuilt.

Today's Reading: Ezekiel 41–43

September

12

And in controversy they shall stand in judgment; and they shall judge it according to my judgments: and they shall keep my laws and my statutes in all mine assemblies; and they shall hallow my sabbaths.

Ezekiel 44:24

During the Millennium the priestly functions will return to the newly built temple.

Today's Reading: Ezekiel 44–45

13

But when the people of the land shall come before the LORD in the solemn feasts, he that entereth in by the way of the north gate to worship shall go out by the way of the south gate; and he that entereth by the way of the south gate shall go forth by the way of the north gate: he shall not return by the way of the gate whereby he came in, but shall go forth over against it.

Ezekiel 46:9

After a person comes to Christ, he must never return to his old life of sin.

Today's Reading: Ezekiel 46–48

September

14

Thou, O king, sawest, and behold a great image. This great image, whose brightness was excellent, stood before thee; and the form thereof was terrible.

Daniel 2:31

The gold head symbolizes the Babylonian empire, the silver chest and arms symbolizes the Medo-Persian empire, the bronze belly and thighs symbolizes the Grecian empire, and the iron and clay legs and feet symbolizes the Roman empire.

Today's Reading: Daniel 1–2

15

This dream I king Nebuchadnezzar have seen. Now thou, O Belteshazzar, declare the interpretation thereof, forasmuch as all the wise men of my kingdom are not able to make known unto me the interpretation: but thou art able; for the spirit of the holy gods is in thee.

Daniel 4:18

God warned King Nebuchadnezzar to repent of his sinful ways; otherwise, He would have him live and eat like a cow, which is eventually what happened to him.

Today's Reading: Daniel 3–4

September

16

And now the wise men, the astrologers, have been brought in before me, that they should read this writing, and make known unto me the interpretation thereof: but they could not shew the interpretation of the thing:

Daniel 5:15

Do not put your faith in astrology because eventually you will be sorry you did.

> Today's Reading: Daniel 5–6

17

And it came to pass, when I, even I Daniel, had seen the vision, and sought for the meaning, then, behold, there stood before me as the appearance of a man.

Daniel 8:15

In Daniel's vision, the angel Gabriel tells Daniel what the last days will be like.

> Today's Reading: Daniel 7–8

September

18

Therefore I was left alone, and saw this great vision, and there remained no strength in me: for my comeliness was turned in me into corruption, and I retained no strength.
Daniel 10:8

Only Daniel was able to see the vision of Jesus Christ, which was so awesome it zapped Daniel of his strength.

> Today's Reading: Daniel 9–10

19

And from the time that the daily sacrifice shall be taken away, and the abomination that maketh desolate set up, there shall be a thousand two hundred and ninety days.
Daniel 12:11

During the Tribulation period the Antichrist will demand that people worship him and not God.

> Today's Reading: Daniel 11–12

September

20

Come, and let us return unto the LORD: for he hath torn, and he will heal us; he hath smitten, and he will bind us up. After two days will he revive us: in the third day he will raise us up, and we shall live in his sight.

Hosea 6:1–2

America needs revival. We need to look to the Lord to heal us of *all* of our problems.

Today's Reading: Hosea 1–6

21

As for Ephraim, their glory shall fly away like a bird, from the birth, and from the womb, and from the conception. Though they bring up their children, yet will I bereave them, that there shall not be a man left: yea, woe also to them when I depart from them!

Hosea 9:11–12

The Lord punished Ephraim for being murderers. If America does not punish murderers, then the Lord will punish our nation.

Today's Reading: Hosea 7–12

September

22

Tell ye your children of it, and let your children tell their children, and their children another generation. That which the palmerworm hath left hath the locust eaten; and that which the locust hath left hath the cankerworm eaten; and that which the cankerworm hath left hath the caterpiller eaten.
Joel 1:3-4

Locust invasions may be signs of judgments against nations that have turned their backs on God.

> Today's Reading: Hosea 13–14, Joel 1–3

23

Will a lion roar in the forest, when he hath no prey? will a young lion cry out of his den, if he have taken nothing? Can a bird fall in a snare upon the earth, where no gin is for him? shall one take up a snare from the earth, and have taken nothing at all?
Amos 3:4-5

We must follow the ways of the Lord; otherwise, we will be as birds caught in the traps of Satan.

> Today's Reading: Amos 1–5

September

24

And though they hide themselves in the top of Carmel, I will search and take them out thence; and though they be hid from my sight in the bottom of the sea, thence will I command the serpent, and he shall bite them:
Amos 9:3

God is omnipresent—He is everywhere.

> Today's Reading: Amos 6–9, Obadiah 1

25

I will surely assemble, O Jacob, all of thee; I will surely gather the remnant of Israel; I will put them together as the sheep of Bozrah, as the flock in the midst of their fold...Their king shall pass before them, and the LORD on the head of them.
Micah 2:12-13

One day soon, God will once again establish His kingdom in Israel.

> Today's Reading: Jonah 1–4, Micah 1–2

September

26

And I will execute vengeance in anger and fury upon the heathen, such as they have not heard.

Micah 5:15

God will one day punish all the evil nations for the sins they have committed, and He will curse them with the curses written in the Bible.

Today's Reading: Micah 3–7

27

Shall not all these take up a parable against him, and a taunting proverb against him, and say, Woe to him that increaseth that which is not his! how long? and to him that ladeth himself with thick clay!

Habakkuk 2:6

God will bring down a proud man unless he repents from his sin.

Today's Reading: Nahum 1–3, Habakkuk 1–3

September

28

And I called for a drought upon the land, and upon the mountains, and upon the corn, and upon the new wine, and upon the oil, and upon that which the ground bringeth forth, and upon men, and upon cattle, and upon all the labour of the hands.

Haggai 1:11

Besides locusts, droughts may also be signs of judgments brought by God against nations and their people.

> Today's Reading: Zephaniah 1–3, Haggai 1–2

29

Then said he, These are the two anointed ones, that stand by the LORD of the whole earth.

Zechariah 4:14

The two anointed ones refer to Joshua, the high priest, and Zerubbabel, the governor. Both offices are separate, but both are still under the authority of *God* and designed to serve *God*.

> Today's Reading: Zechariah 1–6

September

30

But I scattered them with a whirlwind among all the nations whom they knew not. Thus the land was desolate after them, that no man passed through nor returned: for they laid the pleasant land desolate.
Zechariah 7:14

The Jews rebelled against God for 70 years. As a result, God punished them by leaving their land uninhabited and holding them in captivity for the next 70 years.

Today's Reading: Zechariah 7–10

OCTOBER

1

And it shall come to pass in that day, that a great tumult from the LORD shall be among them; and they shall lay hold every one on the hand of his neighbour, and his hand shall rise up against the hand of his neighbour.

Zechariah 14:13

In the last days armies from around the world will surround Jerusalem to attack the city, but God will bring a plague upon these armies, and they will attack and destroy each other.

Today's Reading: Zechariah 11–14

October

2

And now, I pray you, beseech God that he will be gracious unto us: this hath been by your means: will he regard your persons? saith the LORD of hosts.

Malachi 1:9

We should always give God our best, especially when giving our offerings to the Lord.

Today's Reading: Malachi 1–4

3

And being warned of God in a dream that they should not return to Herod, they departed into their own country another way.

Matthew 2:12

The wise men came from the east to Bethlehem bearing gifts for the baby Jesus. Herod tried to deceive the wise men so that he could kill the baby.

Today's Reading: Matthew 1–4

October

4

Wherefore, if God so clothe the grass of the field, which to day is, and to morrow is cast into the oven, shall he not much more clothe you, O ye of little faith?

Matthew 6:30

The Sermon on the Mount teaches us more than just how to live. It teaches us how to live for Jesus.

> Today's Reading: Matthew 5–6

5

That it might be fulfilled which was spoken by Esaias the prophet, saying, Himself took our infirmities, and bare our sicknesses.

Matthew 8:17

Jesus not only took away our sins when he sacrificed himself upon the cross, but he also took our place upon the cross. This holy sacrifice now allows those who are in Christ to stand in God's holy presence.

> Today's Reading: Matthew 7–9

October

6

Now when John had heard in the prison the works of Christ, he sent two of his disciples, And said unto him, Art thou he that should come, or do we look for another?

Matthew 11:2-3

People are still asking that same question today. By the way, who do you say that Jesus is?

Today's Reading: Matthew 10–12

7

And the disciples came, and said unto him, Why speakest thou unto them in parables?

Matthew 13:10

Jesus spoke in parables because he knew that storytelling is one of the best methods for teaching people.

Today's Reading: Matthew 13–14

October

8

And Jesus rebuked the devil; and he departed out of him: and the child was cured from that very hour.

Matthew 17:18

Can a person be filled with the Devil? Not if he has been filled with the Holy Spirit. The apostle John said, "Greater is he that is in you, than he that is in the world" (I John 4:4).

> Today's Reading: Matthew 15–17

9

So the last shall be first, and the first last: for many be called, but few chosen.

Matthew 20:16

The parable of the vineyard portrays how all that come to Christ—no matter how old they were when they accepted Jesus as their Lord and Savior—shall inherit eternal life.

> Today's Reading: Matthew 18–20

October

10

Jesus answered and said unto them, Verily I say unto you, If ye have faith, and doubt not, ye shall not only do this which is done to the fig tree, but also if ye shall say unto this mountain, Be thou removed, and be thou cast into the sea; it shall be done.

Matthew 21:21

God always answers our prayers. The answer may not be what we expected, but it is always the right answer.

Today's Reading: Matthew 21–22

11

Woe unto you, scribes and Pharisees, hypocrites! for ye are like unto whited sepulchres, which indeed appear beautiful outward, but are within full of dead men's bones, and of all uncleanness.

Matthew 23:27

You must do more than just memorize scripture verses. You must also show your love to others; otherwise, you will appear to be alive on the outside, but inside you are dead.

Today's Reading: Matthew 23–24

October

12

Then shall the righteous answer him, saying, Lord, when saw we thee an hungred, and fed thee? or thirsty, and gave thee drink? When saw we thee a stranger, and took thee in? or naked, and clothed thee? Or when saw we thee sick, or in prison, and came unto thee?

Matthew 25:37-39

Jesus said that any time we help someone in need it is as if we have helped Him.

Today's Reading: Matthew 25–26

13

He is not here: for he is risen, as he said. Come, see the place where the Lord lay.

Matthew 28:6

The resurrection is what the New Testament is based upon. Had Jesus not risen from the grave, it would have proven that He was just an ordinary man.

Today's Reading: Matthew 27–28

October

14

But he that shall blaspheme against the Holy Ghost hath never forgiveness, but is in danger of eternal damnation:

Mark 3:29

When a person has no remorse for his sins and rejects Jesus as his deliverer, then he commits blasphemy against the Holy Spirit. As a result, a person sends himself to hell.

> **Today's Reading: Mark 1–3**

15

And all the devils besought him, saying, Send us into the swine, that we may enter into them.

Mark 5:12

The demons recognized who Jesus was, and they knew he had the power to throw them into eternal darkness. Moreover, these demons would have rather lived in swine than go to hell. On the other hand, the swine would rather die than be possessed by demons.

> **Today's Reading: Mark 4–5**

October

16

And she answered and said unto him, Yes, Lord: yet the dogs under the table eat of the children's crumbs. And he said unto her, For this saying go thy way; the devil is gone out of thy daughter.

Mark 7:28-29

Although the woman felt she was not worthy of Jesus, she still begged Him to heal her daughter because she loved her so much. This story reminds us to pray without ceasing.

> Today's Reading: Mark 6–7

17

And his raiment became shining, exceeding white as snow; so as no fuller on earth can white them.

Mark 9:3

Those who have been cleansed by the blood of Jesus will one day be given robes to wear that are whiter than snow.

> Today's Reading: Mark 8–9

October

18

And when he heard that it was Jesus of Nazareth, he began to cry out, and say, Jesus, thou Son of David, have mercy on me.

Mark 10:47

Bartimaeus, the blind beggar, kept crying out to Jesus when he heard it was Jesus passing by. The crowds told him to be quiet, but he cried out all the more. What is it that you need Jesus to fix? Have you cried out to him?

Today's Reading: Mark 10–11

19

And when Jesus saw that he answered discreetly, he said unto him, Thou art not far from the kingdom of God. And no man after that durst ask him any question.

Mark 12:34

To love God with every fiber of our being means more to Jesus than our sacrifices and offerings.

Today's Reading: Mark 12–13

October

20

And he said unto them, Go ye into all the world, and preach the gospel to every creature.

Mark 16:15

Pray for people in other nations and for the Christian missionaries that serve them.

> Today's Reading: Mark 14–16

21

And thou, child, shalt be called the prophet of the Highest: for thou shalt go before the face of the Lord to prepare his ways;

Luke 1:76

John the Baptist's ministry was to preach repentance and to introduce the world to Jesus the Son of God. What has God asked you to do for Him?

> Today's Reading: Luke 1

October

22

And he came into all the country about Jordan, preaching the baptism of repentance for the remission of sins;

Luke 3:3

Water baptism is an ordinance of the church that reminds us that the blood of Jesus Christ—our blessed redeemer—has washed away our sins.

> Today's Reading: Luke 2–3

23

And he charged him to tell no man: but go, and shew thyself to the priest, and offer for thy cleansing, according as Moses commanded, for a testimony unto them.

Luke 5:14

Jesus ordered the man healed of leprosy to go and give the offering required under the Mosaic Law. This is one example of how Jesus came, not to end the law, but to fulfill it.

> Today's Reading: Luke 4–5

October

24

For a good tree bringeth not forth corrupt fruit; neither doth a corrupt tree bring forth good fruit.

Luke 6:43

The type of fruit you bear is found within your heart. Either your fruit is good or it is evil.

Today's Reading: Luke 6–7

25

And Joanna the wife of Chuza Herod's steward, and Susanna, and many others, which ministered unto him of their substance.

Luke 8:3

Jesus sometimes relied on others to provide for his physical needs. This reminds us that He left the throne of glory and became poor to fellowship among us.

Today's Reading: Luke 8

October

26

Let these sayings sink down into your ears: for the Son of man shall be delivered into the hands of men.
                                                    Luke 9:44

Jesus in one way or another is in the first verse of Genesis, and all the way through the Bible to the last verse of Revelation.

> **Today's Reading: Luke 9**

27

But if I with the finger of God cast out devils, no doubt the kingdom of God is come upon you.
                                                    Luke 11:20

Seek the kingdom of God in everything you do and you will be blessed with power from above.

> **Today's Reading: Luke 10–11**

October

28

Or those eighteen, upon whom the tower in Siloam fell, and slew them, think ye that they were sinners above all men that dwelt in Jerusalem?

Luke 13:4

Not everyone that dies in a disaster is guilty of sin. Jesus said the sun rises on the evil and on the good, and sends rain on the just and on the unjust (Matthew 5:45, the author's paraphrase).

> Today's Reading: Luke 12–13

29

It was meet that we should make merry, and be glad: for this thy brother was dead, and is alive again; and was lost, and is found.

Luke 15:32

So many of us are just like the prodigal son. We try so hard to live the way the world does, instead of doing things that are pleasing to God.

> Today's Reading: Luke 14–16

October

30

Take heed to yourselves: If thy brother trespass against thee, rebuke him; and if he repent, forgive him.

Luke 17:3

Jesus said that if a person sins against you many times and is truly repentant each time for what he has done, then it is a Christians' duty to forgive him every single time.

> **Today's Reading: Luke 17–18**

31

Is it lawful for us to give tribute unto Caesar, or no?

Luke 20:22

Two points Jesus made concerning taxes:
1. Everything belongs to God, including taxes.
2. Governments are to be good stewards of what rightfully belongs to God.

> **Today's Reading: Luke 19–20**

NOVEMBER

1

Art thou the Christ? tell us. And he said unto them, If I tell you, ye will not believe:

Luke 22:67

Jesus is either the Son of God or a liar. Each person must decide for himself.

Today's Reading: Luke 21–22

November

2

And he said unto them, These are the words which I spake unto you, while I was yet with you, that all things must be fulfilled, which were written in the law of Moses, and in the prophets, and in the psalms, concerning me.

Luke 24:44

There are at least 44 prophecies of the Messiah found in the Old Testament that have been fulfilled in Jesus Christ. No other person has ever—or will ever—fulfill those prophecies.

Today's Reading: Luke 23–24

3

The wind bloweth where it listeth, and thou hearest the sound thereof, but canst not tell whence it cometh, and whither it goeth: so is every one that is born of the Spirit.

John 3:8

The Spirit is like the wind. Even though we cannot see the wind, we can still feel it. The same is true of the Holy Spirit. Although we cannot see Him, we can still feel Him.

Today's Reading: John 1–3

November

4

How can ye believe, which receive honour one of another, and seek not the honour that cometh from God only?

John 5:44

Honor from God the Father is far more worthy than any prize or award given by man.

> Today's Reading: John 4–5

5

But this people who knoweth not the law are cursed.

John 7:49

You can be a scholar of the Bible and still burn in hell when you die. The Bible is more than just a best-seller. The Holy Book shows the way to eternal life with God the Father through Jesus Christ his Son.

> Today's Reading: John 6–7

November

6

He answered and said, Who is he, Lord, that I might believe on him? And Jesus said unto him, Thou hast both seen him, and it is he that talketh with thee.

John 9:36-37

Jesus healed the blind man, who believed in Him; after death, those who believed in Jesus will also see and talk with Him, face to face.

> **Today's Reading: John 8–9**

7

To him the porter openeth; and the sheep hear his voice: and he calleth his own sheep by name, and leadeth them out.

John 10:3

The world tries to convince people that Jesus does not exist, and if he does exist, then he must be the Devil. But God's people know the truth about Jesus because they know the *Truth*.

> **Today's Reading: John 10–11**

November

8

And there were certain Greeks among them that came up to worship at the feast: The same came therefore to Philip, which was of Bethsaida of Galilee, and desired him, saying, Sir, we would see Jesus. Philip cometh and telleth Andrew: and again Andrew and Philip tell Jesus.

John 12:20-22

Jesus came to the Jews first, and then to the rest of the world. Unfortunately, many people rejected Him back then, and many people still reject Him today.

> **Today's Reading: John 12–13**

9

I came forth from the Father, and am come into the world: again, I leave the world, and go to the Father.

John 16:28

The entire Bible is based upon Jesus' resurrection. However, if the resurrection had not occurred, then the Bible would be a fictional book.

> **Today's Reading: John 14–16**

November

10

Then cried they all again, saying, Not this man, but Barabbas. Now Barabbas was a robber.

John 18:40

The people passed on Jesus—who was without sin—for Barabbas, a thief and murderer.

Today's Reading: John 17–18

11

And seeth two angels in white sitting, the one at the head, and the other at the feet, where the body of Jesus had lain.

John 20:12

Those who believe in Christ will one day meet the angels in heaven. What a day that will be!

Today's Reading: John 19–21

November

12

And they were all filled with the Holy Ghost, and began to speak with other tongues, as the Spirit gave them utterance.
Acts 2:4

The baptism in the Holy Ghost empowers the believer to do God's work.

> Today's Reading: Acts 1–3

13

And the word of God increased; and the number of the disciples multiplied in Jerusalem greatly; and a great company of the priests were obedient to the faith.
Acts 6:7

When trusted members of the church complete the administrative tasks of the church, it allows the pastor more time to pray and do the work of the Lord. This is a key factor in church growth.

> Today's Reading: Acts 4–6

November

14

As for Saul, he made havock of the church, entering into every house, and haling men and women committed them to prison.
Acts 8:3

Like Paul, many individuals over the past 2,000 years have persecuted the church before becoming a Christian.

Today's Reading: Acts 7–8

15

And Saul, yet breathing out threatenings and slaughter against the disciples of the Lord, went unto the high priest, And desired of him letters to Damascus to the synagogues, that if he found any of this way, whether they were men or women, he might bring them bound unto Jerusalem.
Acts 9:1-2

God—out of His gentle mercy—rebukes us on our own Damascus roads and allows us to see the errors of our ways.

Today's Reading: Acts 9–10

November

16

Then remembered I the word of the Lord, how that he said, John indeed baptized with water; but ye shall be baptized with the Holy Ghost.

Acts 11:16

Every born-again believer is baptized only once by the Holy Spirit into the body of Christ (I Corinthian 12:13), but there are many fillings of the Holy Spirit (Ephesians 5:18).

> Today's Reading: Acts 11–13

17

It seemed good unto us, being assembled with one accord, to send chosen men unto you with our beloved Barnabas and Paul, Men that have hazarded their lives for the name of our Lord Jesus Christ.

Acts 15:25-26

The power of God changed the apostles from cowards to fearless men of God who were now ready to die for the cause of Christ if necessary.

> Today's Reading: Acts 14–16

November

18

These were more noble than those in Thessalonica, in that they received the word with all readiness of mind, and searched the scriptures daily, whether those things were so.
Acts 17:11

After listening to a person teach or preach the Word of God, go back and study the Scriptures. Determine if the things taught or preached are true. Also, read, study, and meditate upon the Bible everyday.

Today's Reading: Acts 17–18

19

I have shewed you all things, how that so labouring ye ought to support the weak, and to remember the words of the Lord Jesus, how he said, It is more blessed to give than to receive.
Acts 20:35

Paul reiterates the teachings of Jesus Christ and reminds us that it is far better to give to the needy than to horde our money.

Today's Reading: Acts 19–20

November

20

For thou shalt be his witness unto all men of what thou hast seen and heard.

Acts 22:15

Like Paul, we are to tell others what God has done for us. An honest testimony can inspire others to seek God and His ways.

Today's Reading: Acts 21–22

21

And they neither found me in the temple disputing with any man, neither raising up the people, neither in the synagogues, nor in the city: Neither can they prove the things whereof they now accuse me.

Acts 24:12-13

The Devil will use false accusations to try to stop a Christian from witnessing to others. If a Christian is truly doing the work of God, then the Devil will continue to lack the proof needed in finding sin in a Christian's work.

Today's Reading: Acts 23–25

November

22

And when we were all fallen to the earth, I heard a voice speaking unto me, and saying in the Hebrew tongue, Saul, Saul, why persecutest thou me? it is hard for thee to kick against the pricks.

Acts 26:14

The road to Damascus is where Saul the persecutor became Paul the apostle.

Today's Reading: Acts 26–28

23

And even as they did not like to retain God in their knowledge, God gave them over to a reprobate mind, to do those things which are not convenient;

Romans 1:28

Paul warns that a person mired in sin will forsake God and continue to enjoy committing sins. Paul further states that the carnal mind is enmity against God; it does not submit to God, nor can it do so (Romans 8:7, the author's paraphrase).

Today's Reading: Romans 1–3

November

24

What shall we say then? Is the law sin? God forbid. Nay, I had not known sin, but by the law: for I had not known lust, except the law had said, Thou shalt not covet.

Romans 7:7

The Ten Commandments define what sin is. Therefore, the Law of Moses is good for us, but the grace of Jesus Christ is even better for us.

> Today's Reading: Romans 4–7

25

That if thou shalt confess with thy mouth the Lord Jesus, and shalt believe in thine heart that God hath raised him from the dead, thou shalt be saved.

Romans 10:9

Paul says that if a man truly believes in his heart that Jesus Christ is his Lord and Savior, then he will gladly proclaim this to others.

> Today's Reading: Romans 8–10

November

26

For he is the minister of God to thee for good. But if thou do that which is evil, be afraid; for he beareth not the sword in vain: for he is the minister of God, a revenger to execute wrath upon him that doeth evil.
Romans 13:4

When a person is guilty of a crime, the sentence given to him should be to punish and more importantly to bring that person back into a saving relationship with Jesus Christ.

Today's Reading: Romans 11–14

27

And I am sure that, when I come unto you, I shall come in the fulness of the blessing of the gospel of Christ.
Romans 15:29

Does your church have a benevolence program to help feed the homeless? Find out what you can do to help or to get one started. If necessary, you may be able to work with other churches to get a food pantry started in your area. This is a good way to minister to the poor.

Today's Reading: Romans 15–16

November

28

For I think that God hath set forth us the apostles last, as it were appointed to death: for we are made a spectacle unto the world, and to angels, and to men.

I Corinthians 4:9

Unfortunately, Christians are still a spectacle to the rest of the world, but Paul reminds us: "Do not be ashamed of the gospel of Jesus Christ, because it is the power of God for the salvation of everyone who believes" (Romans 1:16).

> **Today's Reading: I Corinthians 1–4**

29

Therefore let us keep the feast, not with old leaven, neither with the leaven of malice and wickedness; but with the unleavened bread of sincerity and truth.

I Corinthians 5:8

The church must discipline with love those who are guilty of living together out of wedlock. Couples like this may be coming to church not realizing the seriousness of their sin.

> **Today's Reading: I Corinthians 5–8**

November

30

For it is written in the law of Moses, Thou shalt not muzzle the mouth of the ox that treadeth out the corn. Doth God take care for oxen?

I Corinthians 9:9

Every church should make it its number one goal of having at least one full-time pastor who is paid a full-time salary.

> **Today's Reading: I Corinthians 9–11**

DECEMBER

1

And though I have the gift of prophecy, and understand all mysteries, and all knowledge; and though I have all faith, so that I could remove mountains, and have not charity, I am nothing.

I Corinthians 13:2

Exercise the spiritual gift that God has blessed you with, and do it with love.

Today's Reading: I Corinthians 12–14

December

2

Now I will come unto you, when I shall pass through Macedonia: for I do pass through Macedonia.
I Corinthians 16:5

Contact a missionary your church supports and find out how you can help him and his family to continue to do God's work.

Today's Reading: I Corinthians 15–16

3

In whom the god of this world hath blinded the minds of them which believe not, lest the light of the glorious gospel of Christ, who is the image of God, should shine unto them.
II Corinthians 4:4

We must not hide the light of Jesus Christ from this dark world; we need to let His light keep on shining down upon us by doing His will.

Today's Reading: II Corinthians 1–4

December

4

O ye Corinthians, our mouth is open unto you, our heart is enlarged.

II Corinthians 6:11

Be sure to tell others in your town about the *Good News* of Jesus Christ.

Today's Reading: II Corinthians 5–8

5

Examine yourselves, whether ye be in the faith; prove your own selves. Know ye not your own selves, how that Jesus Christ is in you, except ye be reprobates?

II Corinthians 13:5

Are your heart and thoughts pleasing to God? If not, then ask the Holy Spirit to cleanse your heart and mind from the sin in your life. Remember that Jesus Christ lives in you, and He does not like a filthy home.

Today's Reading: II Corinthians 9–13

December

6

For ye have heard of my conversation in time past in the Jews' religion, how that beyond measure I persecuted the church of God, and wasted it:

Galatians 1:13

We must follow Jesus' example and win the hearts of those who persecute the New Testament church of Jesus Christ.

> Today's Reading: Galatians 1–6

7

If ye have heard of the dispensation of the grace of God which is given me to you-ward: How that by revelation he made known unto me the mystery; (as I wrote afore in few words, Whereby, when ye read, ye may understand my knowledge in the mystery of Christ)

Ephesians 3:2-4

God revealed his plan of salvation to Paul, so that Paul could share this mystery with a lost and dying world.

> Today's Reading: Ephesians 1–3

December

8

And take the helmet of salvation, and the sword of the Spirit, which is the word of God:

Ephesians 6:17

Put on the whole armor of God and always be ready to defend your faith in God.

Today's Reading: Ephesians 4–6

9

For indeed he was sick nigh unto death: but God had mercy on him; and not on him only, but on me also, lest I should have sorrow upon sorrow.

Philippians 2:27

Pray that God will have mercy on those who are ill, especially those that are in need of salvation.

Today's Reading: Philippians 1–4

December

10

That their hearts might be comforted, being knit together in love, and unto all riches of the full assurance of understanding, to the acknowledgement of the mystery of God, and of the Father, and of Christ; In whom are hid all the treasures of wisdom and knowledge.

Colossians 2:2-3

Seek the Lord Jesus Christ; you will find the treasures of wisdom, knowledge, and understanding.

Today's Reading: Colossians 1–4

11

Paul, and Silvanus, and Timotheus, unto the church of the Thessalonians which is in God the Father and in the Lord Jesus Christ: Grace be unto you, and peace, from God our Father, and the Lord Jesus Christ.

I Thessalonians 1:1

Paul, Silvanus, and Timothy wrote this letter to the church in Thessalonica during the 1st century AD. However, these letters are just as powerful for our modern-day churches.

Today's Reading: I Thessalonians 1–5

December

12

But we are bound to give thanks alway to God for you, brethren beloved of the Lord, because God hath from the beginning chosen you to salvation through sanctification of the Spirit and belief of the truth:

II Thessalonians 2:13

In the song *What a Friend We Have in Jesus,* we are reminded to "take it (everything) to the Lord in prayer."

> Today's Reading: II Thessalonians 1–3

13

A bishop then must be blameless, the husband of one wife, vigilant, sober, of good behaviour, given to hospitality, apt to teach;

I Timothy 3:2

A true minister of God will practice what he preaches, which is a godly lifestyle lead by the Holy Spirit.

> Today's Reading: I Timothy 1–4

December

14

Concerning the wealthy,...they should be laying up in store for themselves a good foundation against the time to come, that they may lay hold on eternal life.

I Timothy 6:17, 19

Store up for yourselves a good foundation in heaven and put your faith in God who provides true riches.

> **Today's Reading: I Timothy 5–6**

15

I charge thee therefore before God, and the Lord Jesus Christ, who shall judge the quick and the dead at his appearing and his kingdom; Preach the word; be instant in season, out of season; reprove, rebuke, exhort with all longsuffering and doctrine.

II Timothy 4:1-2

Carnal Christians do not want to hear sound doctrine; if necessary they go from church to church until they find a worldly church that tells them what their itchy ears want to hear (2 Timothy 4:4, the author's paraphrase).

> **Today's Reading: II Timothy 1–4**

December

16

I thank my God, making mention of thee always in my prayers,

Philemon 1:4

We should pray daily for those who partake of the Lord's work.

> Today's Reading: Titus 1–3, Philemon 1

17

For unto us was the gospel preached, as well as unto them: but the word preached did not profit them, not being mixed with faith in them that heard it.

Hebrews 4:2

Hearing the Word preached is not enough; you must have faith that what you are hearing is the truth.

> Today's Reading: Hebrews 1–5

December

18

And we desire that every one of you do shew the same diligence to the full assurance of hope unto the end:

Hebrews 6:11

Ask the Lord to help you to be more faithful and patient when witnessing to others.

Today's Reading: Hebrews 6–9

19

And every priest standeth daily ministering and offering oftentimes the same sacrifices, which can never take away sins:

Hebrews 10:11

Nobody can take away another person's sins; only Jesus can take away our sins.

Today's Reading: Hebrews 10–11

December

20

For whom the Lord loveth he chasteneth, and scourgeth every son whom he receiveth.

Hebrews 12:6

The Lord disciplines those He loves (Proverbs 3:12, the author's paraphrase).

> Today's Reading: Hebrews 12–13

21

Wherefore, my beloved brethren, let every man be swift to hear, slow to speak, slow to wrath: For the wrath of man worketh not the righteousness of God.

James 1:19-20

Many conflicts could possibly be avoided if we just follow these three simple rules:
1. Be swift to hear.
2. Be slow to speak.
3. Be slow to wrath.

> Today's Reading: James 1–5

December

22

As every man hath received the gift, even so minister the same one to another, as good stewards of the manifold grace of God.
I Peter 4:10

Good stewardship is managing God's resources well such as our money, food, clothes, homes, and families.

> **Today's Reading: I Peter 1–5**

23

For he received from God the Father honour and glory, when there came such a voice to him from the excellent glory, This is my beloved Son, in whom I am well pleased. And this voice which came from heaven we heard, when we were with him in the holy mount.
II Peter 1:17-18

Peter is referring to the transfiguration of Jesus in which he witnessed Jesus speaking with Moses and Elijah. This is further proof of life after death.

> **Today's Reading: II Peter 1–3**

December

24

For this is the love of God, that we keep his commandments: and his commandments are not grievous.

I John 5:3

If we love God, then we will obey His commandments, and if we obey His commandments then we will have peace in our hearts.

> Today's Reading: I John 1–5

25

If there come any unto you, and bring not this doctrine, receive him not into your house, neither bid him God speed:

II John 1:10

Beware of those individuals who claim to know the Bible, but *deny* the work of Jesus Christ, His suffering on the cross, and especially His resurrection.

> Today's Reading: II John 1, III John 1, Jude 1

December

26

He that overcometh, the same shall be clothed in white raiment; and I will not blot out his name out of the book of life, but I will confess his name before my Father, and before his angels.

Revelation 3:5

The white clothes symbolize our cleansing from sin. When a *believer* dies, he is clothed in white and stands in the presence of God.

Today's Reading: Revelation 1–3

27

And when he had opened the second seal, I heard the second beast say, Come and see. And there went out another horse that was red: and power was given to him that sat thereon to take peace from the earth, and that they should kill one another: and there was given unto him a great sword.

Revelation 6:3-4

Until Jesus comes we will continue to have wars and bloodshed, but we should try to live in peace with all men if at all possible.

Today's Reading: Revelation 4–8

December

28

And when the seven thunders had uttered their voices, I was about to write: and I heard a voice from heaven saying unto me, Seal up those things which the seven thunders uttered, and write them not.

Revelation 10:4

What did the seven thunders say? We do not know because this is a mystery of God, and we will have to wait to find out.

> **Today's Reading: Revelation 9–12**

29

And the beast which I saw was like unto a leopard, and his feet were as the feet of a bear, and his mouth as the mouth of a lion: and the dragon gave him his power, and his seat, and great authority.

Revelation 13:2

After the Devil, the Beast, and the False Prophet are thrown into the lake of fire, they will be tormented throughout eternity.

> **Today's Reading: Revelation 13–16**

December

30

And I heard as it were the voice of a great multitude, and as the voice of many waters, and as the voice of mighty thunderings, saying, Alleluia: for the Lord God omnipotent reigneth.

Revelation 19:6

Corporate prayer can be so powerful it sounds like a roaring waterfall.

Today's Reading: Revelation 17–19

31

And God shall wipe away all tears from their eyes; and there shall be no more death, neither sorrow, nor crying, neither shall there be any more pain: for the former things are passed away.

Revelation 21:4

You *must* be a Christian in order to get into heaven. It is a place where there are no more tears, death, sorrow, or pain.

Today's Reading: Revelation 20–22

Book Rev. Casaus as a Speaker

Learn to Teach Like the Master.

- Learn the 5 secrets to great teaching
- Discover how to increase attendance in your classes
- Make Jesus' master plan your master plan
- Gain knowledge on how to prepare effective lesson plans
- Acquire the skills you need to teach like a professional

Filled with knowledge and Godly wisdom, Rev. Casaus is a polished and experienced speaker that connects with audiences of every age. He also teaches at both high school and college levels. Rev. Casaus provides attendees who want to teach like professionals to high schoolers, college age or adults, to leave with a personal vision for goals, tactics, and the motivation to be and build better disciples for tomorrow.

Pastors, associate pastors, small group leaders, and those who teach Bible studies to high school students up to adults will benefit from Rev. Casaus' teaching.

CONTACT
To schedule Rev. Casaus, visit **bridanpublishing.com**

And they shall not teach every man his neighbour, and every man his brother, saying, Know the Lord: for all shall know me, from the least to the greatest.
- Hebrews 8:11

Book Rev. Casaus to Preach at Your Church

Read, Heed, and Succeed

Brother Casaus delivers a powerful sermon on what it means to be successful in the eyes of the LORD and how individuals can achieve this success. His is not a pie in the sky myth, but a compelling message about how to put your trust in God and obey Him in order to reap His blessings. Brother Casaus teaches how God calls, commissions and comforts those who are willing to serve Him. Contact us today to let Rev. Casaus serve you and your congregation.

CONTACT
To schedule Rev. Casaus, visit **bridanpublishing.com**

And they shall not teach every man his neighbour, and every man his brother, saying, Know the Lord: for all shall know me, from the least to the greatest.
- *Hebrews 8:11*

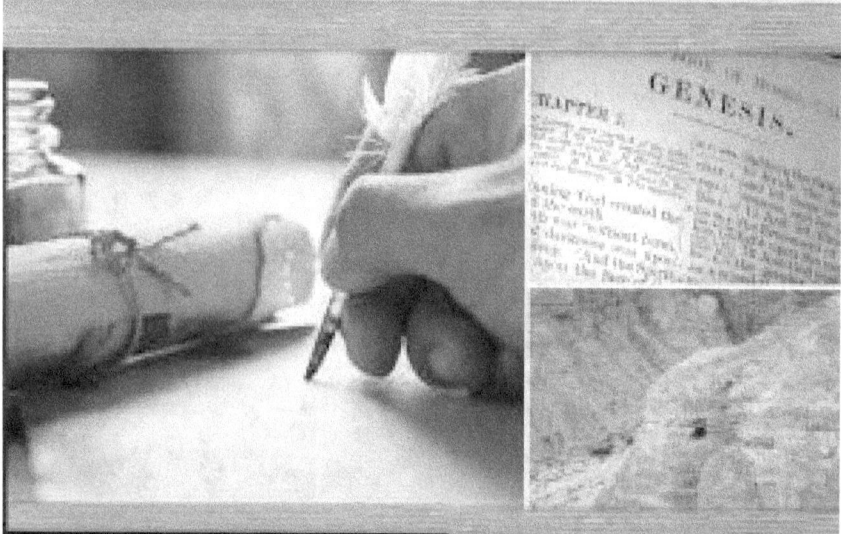

DAILY BIBLE STUDY 101:
Bible Outlines

Reggie Casaus

A great companion to
Daily Bible Study 101: Daily Devotional

- Over 7,000 multiple choice questions and answers
- Daily reading plans
- And more! Designed to help you dig deep and allow the Word to take root in your heart and mind

Available at most local and online bookstores.

About the Author

Reverend Reggie Casaus is a graduate of Berean School of the Bible. Filled with knowledge and Godly wisdom, Rev. Casaus is a polished and experienced speaker, teacher, ordained pastor and author that connects with audiences of every age. He has taught at both high school and college levels, at Bearden High School in Knoxville, Tennessee and Roane State Community College in Harriman, Tennessee. Daily Bible Study 101: Daily Devotional *is his second book, and companion to his first,* Daily Bible Study 101: Questions & Answers. *Both volumes are available in local and online bookstores. Reach Rev. Casaus at* **bridanpublishing.com**

www.ingramcontent.com/pod-product-compliance
Lightning Source LLC
Chambersburg PA
CBHW070549010526
44118CB00012B/1269